It's Not Defiance

Why Your Child Shuts Down,
Melts Down, or Checks Out

A Parent's Guide to Demand Sensitivity

Rachelle Manco, LCSW

Justin Manco, CMHC

BSPUTAH, LLC

Copyright

Published by BSPUTAH, LLC.

This book is not a substitute for professional medical or mental health advice, diagnosis, or treatment. Always seek the advice of a qualified professional with any questions regarding a medical or psychological condition. If you or your child are in crisis, call 988 (Suicide and Crisis Lifeline), text HOME to 741741 (Crisis Text Line), or go to your nearest emergency room.

ISBN: 979-8-9952881-4-5

Second Edition

Printed in the United States of America.

relatepda.com

Contents

Welcome

This book is for you if you are in the daily work of supporting someone whose nervous system responds to everyday demands as threats.

That might mean you are a parent, a stepparent, a grandparent, a foster parent, a partner, or any other person who shows up every day in a support role. The specific title does not matter. What matters is that you are here, that you are probably exhausted, and that nothing you have tried so far has worked the way it was supposed to.

The reward charts did not work. The consequences did not work. The gentle parenting scripts did not work. The therapist who said "hold firmer boundaries" did not work. None of it worked because none of it was built for what is actually happening in your child's nervous system.

Your child has what we call demand sensitivity. Their brain's threat-detection system responds to everyday demands (get dressed, eat breakfast, put your shoes on, say thank you) the same way most brains respond to physical danger. The response is automatic. It is pre-conscious. It is not a choice. By the time you see the refusal, the meltdown, or the shutdown, their nervous system has already been in survival mode for longer than either of you realized.

The clinical name for this profile is Pathological Demand Avoidance, or PDA. We use both terms in this book. PDA connects you to the research and the community that already exists around this profile. Demand sensitivity describes the mechanism: a nervous system that is more reactive to demands as a stimulus, the same way some nervous systems are more reactive to light, sound, or texture.

This book is built on RELATE, a clinical intervention framework for PDA. It is the first of its kind. RELATE was developed from direct work with neurodivergent individuals in residential treatment and intensive outpatient settings. The environments where demand avoidance is most severe and where standard approaches fail hardest. The full clinical framework, including the research grounding and assessment instruments, is detailed in the RELATE Foundational Training Manual, written for professionals and available at relatepda.com.

This book takes the core of that framework and puts it in your hands. In language that reflects where you actually live, not where clinicians theorize.

A few things this book is, and is not.

It is evidence-informed. It draws on established research in attachment science, Intolerance of Uncertainty, affective neuroscience, polyvagal theory, and trauma-informed care. It is not empirically validated. No randomized controlled trials exist for RELATE or for any PDA intervention approach, anywhere. The entire PDA intervention field is at an early stage. This book is transparent about that because you deserve honesty about what you are working with.

It is not therapy. It is not a substitute for professional mental health support, for your child or for you. If your child is in crisis (expressing thoughts about not wanting to be alive, engaging in self-harm, shutting down so completely that basic safety is at risk) seek professional help now. This book will be here when the immediate crisis has passed.

It is written with the understanding that demand landscapes are shaped by more than individual nervous systems. Race, culture, economic circumstances, gender identity, family structure, and systemic inequity all add layers of demand that compound everything described here. The principles in this book apply across contexts, but the specific demands your family faces may include dimensions not explicitly named in these pages.

All worksheets, reference cards, and printable tools are in the Appendix at the back of the book, organized by chapter. The text will point you to them by name when they are relevant. The body of the book is the conversation. The Appendix is the toolkit.

One more thing. This book will ask you, eventually, to look at your own nervous system. Your regulation. Your patterns. Your burnout. That part comes later, not first. Before we ask anything of you, we are going to explain what is happening in your child, join you in the reality of what you are living with, and give you a framework and a playbook you can use tonight.

PART ONE

What's Happening

PART ONE

Chapter 1: What Is Demand Sensitivity?

Your child's nervous system is different from most. Not broken. Not disordered. Different in a specific way that has a name, a mechanism, and a growing body of research behind it. Once you understand what that difference is, the behavior that has confused you, exhausted you, and made you question your own parenting will start making sense. Not because the behavior changes immediately. Because you will finally know what you are looking at.

You are looking at a nervous system that responds to everyday demands as threats.

Not metaphorical threats. Not "it feels hard." Actual neurological threat responses, produced by the same brain circuitry that responds to physical danger. When you say "put your shoes on," your child's brain may process that sentence the same way it would process a stranger grabbing their arm. The thinking brain goes offline. The survival brain takes over. What you see from the outside is refusal, shutdown, or meltdown. What is happening inside is a nervous system in fight-or-flight over something that looks, to everyone else, completely manageable.

This is what the clinical literature calls Pathological Demand Avoidance, or PDA. We use that term in this book because it is the one most recognized in the research and the community. It is how you will find other families, other professionals, and other resources that understand what you are dealing with.

But we also use another term: demand sensitivity. And the reason matters.

Why "demand sensitivity"

Think about sensory sensitivity. A child with sensory sensitivity has a nervous system that is more reactive to light, sound, texture, or smell. Nobody hears "sensory sensitivity" and thinks the child is choosing to be bothered by the tag in their shirt. Nobody blames them for covering their ears in a loud room. The word "sensitivity" communicates something immediate: this is how the nervous system works. It is not a behavior. It is not a choice. It is a condition of the system.

Demand sensitivity means the same thing, applied to demands as a stimulus. Your child has a nervous system that is more reactive to demands. Not because they are oppositional. Not because they are lazy or defiant or manipulative. Because their brain's threat-detection circuitry responds to demands the way other brains respond to danger. The response is automatic. It happens below conscious awareness. By the time your child knows they are refusing, the refusal has already started.

The word "avoidance" in Pathological Demand Avoidance names what you can see from the outside. The behavior. The visible output. Demand sensitivity names what is happening inside. The nervous system state that produces the behavior. This distinction is not academic. It changes what you do about it. When you name a condition after its most visible behavior, you accidentally invite people to target the behavior. "They are avoidant, so let's work on the avoidance." That is the approach that fails with this population, because the avoidance is not the problem. The nervous system state driving the avoidance is the problem.

Every strategy in this book targets the nervous system state, not the behavior. That is why the strategies work when other approaches have not.

What PDA actually is

PDA was first described by Elizabeth Newson in the 1980s. She was seeing children who did not fit the existing categories. They were autistic, or had strong autistic traits, but their presentation was different from what clinicians expected. These children resisted demands with an intensity and sophistication that went beyond what other frameworks could explain. They used social strategies (charm, distraction, negotiation, excuses) to avoid demands. They could appear highly social on the surface. And the avoidance extended to everything, including things they wanted to do.

Newson named the pattern Pathological Demand Avoidance. The term did its job. It gave clinicians a way to talk about something that had not been talked about before. It opened the door to research, to community, to recognition.

The word "pathological" has not aged well. It implies disease. It implies something fundamentally wrong with the person. For a profile that is increasingly understood as a neurological difference, that word carries weight that most people in the community no longer want it to carry. Other terms have emerged. Pervasive Drive for Autonomy reframes the experience around a strength: the person is not avoiding demands, they are driven toward autonomy. It is empowering language, and for many adults with PDA it resonates deeply. Persistent Demand Avoidance replaces "pathological" with something more neutral.

Each of these terms gets something right. None of them gets everything right. We use PDA because it is the most recognized term and connects you to the existing literature. We use demand sensitivity because it describes the mechanism rather than the behavior and removes the judgment that other terms carry. Both are needed. PDA tells you what the community calls this profile. Demand sensitivity tells you what the nervous system is actually doing.

This is not defiance

The title of this book exists for a reason. The most common thing a PDA parent hears, from teachers, from family, from therapists, from strangers in the grocery store, is some version of: your child is being defiant and you need to be firmer.

That assessment is wrong. Not partially wrong. Completely wrong. And the interventions it produces (consequences, reward charts, behavioral contracts, "consistent boundaries") are not just ineffective for PDA. They make it worse. They add demands to an already overloaded system. They teach the nervous system that the people around it are sources of additional threat, not safety.

Defiance implies choice. It implies that the child has evaluated the demand, decided they do not want to comply, and is refusing as a deliberate act. That sequence requires the thinking brain to be online. It requires the prefrontal cortex, the part of the brain responsible for evaluation, decision-making, and behavioral regulation, to be functioning.

In PDA, the thinking brain is not online when the refusal happens. The threat response has already fired. The amygdala, the brain's alarm system, has already activated. Stress hormones are already flooding the system. The prefrontal cortex has already gone partially or fully offline. The child is not choosing to refuse. The choice was never available.

This is not a subtle distinction. It is the distinction. Everything in this book follows from it.

What demands actually are

When we say "demands," we do not mean only the obvious ones. "Put your shoes on" is a demand. So is "good morning." So is the expectation that your child will sit at the table. So is the look on your face when you are running late. So is the knowledge that something will be asked of them later.

Demands exist in three layers.

Explicit demands are the ones you can hear yourself saying. Get dressed. Do your homework. Say thank you. Come to dinner. These are real, and they add up faster than you think, but they are only the visible layer.

Implicit demands are unstated but expected. The assumption that your child will greet a visitor. The unspoken rule about screen time that has never been formally negotiated but gets enforced when violated. The expectation that they will be in a reasonable mood. Your child's nervous system is tracking these. It knows what you expect even when you have not said it out loud.

Invisible demands are the ones you may not have identified as demands at all. Your body language communicating urgency. The ambient pressure of a tidy house. The social performance expected when grandparents visit. The emotional expectation that they be grateful for something you did for them. The demand to transition from one activity to another. The demand embedded in a question: "How was school?" sounds like small talk. It is actually a request to retrieve, organize, and narrate experience on command.

All three layers register in your child's nervous system. All three contribute to the total demand load. And the nervous system does not distinguish between them. A direct command and an unspoken expectation arrive at the same threat-detection circuitry and produce the same activation.

This is why your child can seem fine for hours and then fall apart over something tiny. The tiny thing was not the cause. It was the last demand in a long series that finally exceeded what the system could hold. The meltdown about socks at 7:45 AM is not about socks. It is about the 47 demands that preceded the socks, most of which nobody counted.

The demand budget

Your child has a finite demand budget that depletes through use and replenishes through recovery. Think of it as a bank account. Every demand, explicit, implicit, and invisible, is a withdrawal. Sleep, safety, autonomy, and regulation are deposits. When the account is empty, even tiny demands produce enormous responses.

The response is not disproportionate. The account is overdrawn.

This reframe changes everything. You stop asking "why are they falling apart over this?" and start asking "what has the total demand load been today?" The answer almost always explains the reaction. The demand that triggered the meltdown is rarely the demand that caused it.

It is the last one in a long line.

Tracking the demand budget across the day, not just individual demands, changes what you see and what you expect. It changes what you ask of your child and when you ask it. It changes how you structure the morning, the evening, the transitions in between. It changes what you consider non-negotiable and what you are willing to release.

The demand audit, which you will learn in Chapter 8, is the tool for making the invisible visible. It takes the three layers of demands and puts them on paper so you can see the actual load your child's nervous system is carrying. Most parents who complete it for the first time are stunned by the number. Not because they are placing too many demands. Because no one ever told them that the demands they considered normal were demands at all.

PART ONE

Chapter 2: The Three Mechanisms

Chapter 1 told you what is happening: your child's nervous system responds to everyday demands as threats. This chapter tells you why. Not in abstract terms. In the specific, concrete, neurological terms that will change how you see your child's behavior from this point forward.

Three mechanisms drive the demand-threat response. They operate together, not in isolation. A single demand can trigger all three simultaneously, which is why the response often seems so far out of proportion to what was asked. It is not one alarm going off. It is three.

Understanding these mechanisms is not optional background information. It is the reason every strategy in this book works. When a strategy does not work, mechanism knowledge tells you why. When your child's response makes no sense, mechanism knowledge makes it make sense. Every time.

Mechanism 1: Subcortical threat detection

Your child's brain has a threat-detection system that operates faster than conscious thought. It is centered in the amygdala, a small structure deep in the brain that processes incoming information and decides, before the thinking brain gets involved, whether something is safe or dangerous.

In most nervous systems, everyday demands pass through this system without triggering a significant response. "Put your shoes on" registers as a task. Annoying, maybe. Boring, possibly. But not dangerous.

In your child's nervous system, "put your shoes on" can register as a threat. The amygdala fires. Stress hormones (norepinephrine, cortisol) flood the brain. The prefrontal cortex, the part of the brain responsible for flexible thinking, problem solving, and behavioral regulation, goes partially or fully offline. The brain shifts from deliberation to defense.

This is not a metaphor. It is a measurable, neurochemical process. Research by Arnsten (2009) established the specific mechanism: elevated stress hormones rapidly impair prefrontal networks while simultaneously strengthening amygdala function. As threat increases, the brain's capacity for flexible, goal-directed behavior decreases. Its capacity for reflexive, defensive behavior increases. The system flips from thinking to surviving.

This flip happens before your child is aware of it. Before they have decided anything. Before they have chosen anything. The threat response is already running by the time they know they are refusing. You cannot reason with this response because the reasoning brain is not available. You cannot talk them through it because the language-processing parts of the brain are running at reduced capacity. You cannot convince them the demand is safe because the part of the brain that evaluates evidence and updates predictions is offline.

This is why logic does not work during a meltdown. This is why "but you did it yesterday" does not register. This is why "just try" lands as another threat on top of the one already firing. The thinking brain is not receiving your input. The survival brain is, and it interprets your persistence as escalation.

What does work: reducing the threat signals the nervous system is encountering. Lowering your voice. Slowing down. Dropping the demand. Giving space. These do not feel like interventions. They feel like giving up. They are the only things that allow the prefrontal cortex to come back online, which is the only way your child regains access to flexible thinking, cooperation, and the ability to do the thing you originally asked.

The entire RELATE framework is built on this sequence: reduce the threat first, then the capacity returns. Not the other way around.

Mechanism 2: Intolerance of Uncertainty

Every demand carries uncertainty. When someone asks you to do something, multiple unknowns are embedded in the ask. Will I be able to do it? How long will it take? What happens if I fail? What comes after this? Is there another demand behind this one?

For most people, these unknowns are tolerable. Background noise. You register them and move on.

For someone with elevated Intolerance of Uncertainty (IU), each unknown is amplified into threat. The uncertainty itself is the danger. Not the feared outcome. The not-knowing.

This distinction matters. Standard anxiety treatment often focuses on helping a person tolerate specific feared outcomes. "What is the worst that could happen? Could you handle that?" That approach assumes the problem is a specific fear that can be examined and reframed. In PDA, the problem is often not a specific fear. It is the uncertainty that surrounds every demand, and no amount of reassurance about specific outcomes resolves it. You address one unknown and three more take its place, because the uncertainty is structural. It is baked into the nature of demands themselves.

Research by Stuart and colleagues (2020) found that Intolerance of Uncertainty was a stronger predictor of PDA traits than anxiety alone. That finding has direct implications for what you do at home. It explains why your child can handle a demand perfectly one day and collapse over the same demand the next: the uncertainty load was different. It explains why open-ended demands ("we'll see," "maybe later," "it depends") are among the most activating things you can say. Each of those phrases is pure uncertainty. The nervous system reads them as danger.

It also explains why predictability is one of the most powerful tools you have. Not rigid schedules. Not compliance structures. Predictability in your behavior. When your child can predict what you will do, because you respond consistently from a regulated state rather than reacting from whatever state you happen to be in, the uncertainty drops. Your predictability is a regulation resource their nervous system can rely on. More on this in Chapter 8 when we cover the Environment pillar.

What IU means in practice: your child is not being difficult about uncertainty. Their nervous system is responding to uncertainty the way yours would respond to standing at the edge of a cliff without a railing. The uncertainty is experienced as physical danger. Reducing it, wherever you can, is not coddling. It is removing a threat.

Mechanism 3: Perceived loss of autonomy

Demands constrain choice. That is what makes them demands. When someone tells you to do something, your options narrow. For most people, this narrowing is experienced as inconvenient. Annoying.

Sometimes frustrating. But tolerable.

For your child, the narrowing of choice is experienced as a survival-level threat. The nervous system responds to the loss of control over their own actions as though their existence is at stake.

This is grounded in research. Deci and Ryan's Self-Determination Theory (2000, 2017) established that perceived autonomy is not merely a preference. It is a fundamental psychological need. When autonomy is absent, wellbeing, motivation, and functioning consistently deteriorate. For PDA nervous systems, this deterioration is not gradual. It is immediate and intense.

This mechanism explains the single most confusing feature of PDA: your child refuses things they want to do.

The child who asked to go to the park cannot get in the car. The teenager who wants to apply for the job cannot open the application. The adult who desperately wants to take a shower cannot make their body walk to the bathroom. The desire is unchanged. The demand character of the activity is what changed. The moment something shifts from "I want to" to "I have to" or even "I should," the threat response activates. Wanting something and being able to tolerate the demands involved in doing it are two different systems. In demand sensitivity, those systems are in direct conflict.

This is the moment most PDA parents recognize their child. If you have watched your child beg for something and then refuse it the moment it becomes available, you have seen this mechanism in action. It is not inconsistency. It is not manipulation. It is two systems (desire and threat detection) producing contradictory outputs, and the threat detection system wins because it operates faster and at a deeper level than conscious wanting.

What this means at home: every interaction is an opportunity to either preserve or threaten autonomy. Offering genuine choices (not "do it now or do it later" but actual options including the option to not do it) preserves autonomy. Framing things as invitations rather than instructions preserves autonomy. Allowing your child control over when, where, and how something happens, even when the "what" is non-negotiable, preserves autonomy. Each of these reduces the threat load of the demand without removing the demand itself.

The word "genuine" is doing a lot of work in that paragraph. Your child's nervous system detects fake choices instantly. "Do you want to put your shoes on now or in five minutes?" when both options end with shoes on is not a genuine choice. It is a demand wearing a question's clothing. Their threat-detection system is designed to identify constraint disguised as choice. That is not a deficit. That is the system working exactly as it was built to work.

The three mechanisms together

These three mechanisms do not take turns. They fire together. A single demand, "time to get ready for school," can simultaneously trigger subcortical threat detection (the demand itself is registered as danger), amplify Intolerance of Uncertainty (what will the morning involve? how many steps? will I be able to do them? what happens if I can't?), and threaten autonomy (I did not choose this, I do not control the timeline, my options just narrowed). Three alarms, one sentence.

This is why the response looks so extreme relative to the demand. You said nine words. Their nervous system processed three simultaneous threat signals, each reinforcing the others. By the time you see the reaction, the system has been in activation for longer than the interaction has been happening.

And here is the part that changes how you parent: if you did not know about these mechanisms, your natural response to the extreme reaction is to add more. More explanation. More reasoning. More urgency. More consequences. Each of those additions is another demand on a system that is already past capacity. You are pouring water into an overflowing cup and wondering why the floor is wet.

Knowing the mechanisms reverses your instincts. Instead of adding, you subtract. Instead of explaining, you go quiet. Instead of insisting, you offer an exit. Instead of tightening control, you hand it back. These responses feel wrong to every instinct you have as a parent. They are right for this nervous system.

Your nervous system is part of this

There is a fourth element operating in every interaction between you and your child, and it is yours.

Nervous systems do not operate in isolation. They talk to each other constantly, through channels that are faster than language: facial expression, muscle tension, vocal pitch, breathing rate, the quality of your attention. Your child's nervous system is reading yours in real time, below conscious awareness, and adjusting its own state in response.

This is called co-regulation. It is not a technique. It is a biological process. It happens automatically, in both directions.

When you are regulated (calm, present, not transmitting urgency or frustration) your child's nervous system encounters something different than when you are activated. It does not read your words. It reads your state. If you are anxious, rushed, frustrated, or performing calm while feeling activated underneath, their system reads the truth. It cannot be fooled.

This is not a guilt trip. You will hear it as one. Almost every parent does. Sit with it for a moment and hear it again: your state is one of the most powerful variables in your child's environment, and it is one of the few variables you can actually change. That makes you the most powerful lever available. Not the problem. The lever.

Think of two tuning forks. Strike one and place it near the other. The second one starts vibrating at the same frequency without being touched. That is co-regulation. Your nervous system is the first tuning fork. When it is vibrating with anxiety, urgency, or frustration, your child's system will match it. When it is steady, their system has a better chance of finding steady too.

We are not going to ask you to work on your regulation right now. That comes in Part 4, after you have the framework and the playbook in hand. But we are naming co-regulation here because it is part of the mechanism. It is part of why the strategies in Part 3 work. A regulated parent implementing RELATE and a dysregulated parent implementing the same strategies produce different results, not because the strategies are different, but because the nervous system delivering them is different.

For now, just know that it exists. Your state matters. Not as judgment. As physics.

Chapter 3: What It Looks Like

You now know the mechanisms. Subcortical threat detection. Intolerance of Uncertainty. Perceived loss of autonomy. Three systems firing together, below conscious awareness, in response to everyday demands.

This chapter shows you what those mechanisms look like when they are operating in your child. Not in clinical language. In the language of your actual life. The morning. The grocery store. The birthday party they planned for a week and then refused to attend. The homework that took four hours of standoff and twelve minutes of actual work.

You will recognize your child in this chapter. That recognition is the point.

Resistance to everyday demands

The most visible feature of demand sensitivity is resistance to things that most children handle without significant difficulty. Getting dressed. Eating meals. Leaving the house. Brushing teeth. Transitioning from one activity to another. Going to bed.

The resistance can be explosive: screaming, crying, throwing things, hitting, running. It can also be invisible: going silent, going limp, staring blankly, walking away, retreating to their room, suddenly feeling sick.

What makes this different from typical childhood resistance is the scope and the intensity. Every child resists demands sometimes. That is normal. What distinguishes demand sensitivity is that the resistance is pervasive (extending across settings and situations, not limited to one context), persistent (present more days than not, over months and years, not just bad weeks), and it extends to demands the child places on themselves. That last part is critical. A child who does not want to do homework is having a normal day. A child who cannot do the thing they spent all morning saying they wanted to do is showing you something different.

The intensity is also different. A typical power struggle over getting dressed lasts a few minutes and resolves when the child decides it is not worth fighting over. A demand sensitivity response can last an hour. It can escalate to a point that feels dangerous. It does not respond to the tools that end typical resistance: distraction, humor, gentle insistence, consequences, rewards. The tools do not work because they were designed for a different mechanism. They assume the child has access to their thinking brain and is making a cost-benefit calculation. In demand sensitivity, the thinking brain is offline. There is no calculation happening.

Strategic avoidance

Before reaching meltdown, most demand sensitive children deploy a range of strategies to avoid the demand. This is not a conscious decision to manipulate. It is a nervous system using every available tool to reduce a perceived threat. The strategies are often socially sophisticated, which is part of what makes PDA confusing to the people around the child.

Common strategies include: elaborate excuses ("my stomach hurts," "I forgot how," "I already did it"), negotiation and bargaining ("can I do it after this show?" repeated indefinitely), distraction and subject-changing (suddenly asking an unrelated question, starting a different conversation, introducing a new topic with enough energy to derail the original request), charm and humor (making the adult laugh, being suddenly affectionate, performing helpfulness on a different task to avoid the one being asked), role reversal (telling the adult what to do, becoming the director of the interaction to reclaim control), and delay tactics that look like partial compliance (getting one sock on and then stopping, opening the homework binder and then staring at it for forty minutes).

These strategies can look calculated. They are not. They are a threat response deploying whatever tools the nervous system has developed over years of encountering demands it cannot tolerate. The sophistication of the strategies does not indicate conscious manipulation. It indicates a nervous system that has had a lot of practice.

This social fluency is also part of what masks the underlying autism in many PDA children. People assume that a child who can negotiate that skillfully, who can read the room well enough to use charm as an avoidance tool, must be choosing their behavior. That assumption is wrong. The social skills are real. The choice is not.

Surface sociability

Many demand sensitive children can appear highly social. They can be funny, engaging, even charismatic in certain contexts. They may seem comfortable with adults, able to hold a conversation, skilled at reading social dynamics. From the outside, they do not look like children who are struggling.

This surface sociability is genuine in the sense that the social skills are real. It is misleading in the sense that it masks the demand load the child is carrying. Being social is itself a demand. It requires tracking expectations, managing performance, monitoring the other person's reactions, and producing appropriate responses. For a demand sensitive child, social interaction is work, even when they are good at it and even when they enjoy it.

The cost of social performance is paid later. The child who was the life of the party collapses in the car on the way home. The child who was "fine" at school melts down within twenty minutes of walking through the front door. The sociability is real but it is not free. It draws from the same demand budget as everything else.

Intense need for control

This often shows up as needing to direct play, choosing the rules, deciding the plan, dictating who sits where and who does what. It can look bossy. It can look inflexible. It can exhaust other children and frustrate adults who want the child to learn to take turns, share control, and compromise.

From the outside, it looks like a child who always has to have their way. From the inside, it is a nervous system trying to create predictability. When the child controls the situation, the unknowns decrease. The Intolerance of Uncertainty mechanism quiets. The autonomy-threat mechanism quiets. Control is not a preference for these children. It is a regulation strategy. Take it away and you remove the only tool that was keeping the system from activating.

This does not mean you never set limits. It means you understand what is happening when you do. You are not correcting a character flaw. You are removing a regulation tool, and the nervous system will respond accordingly.

Emotional variability

Mood can shift rapidly and intensely. Your child can go from laughing to screaming in minutes. They can be calm and cooperative at 3:00 and completely unreachable at 3:15. They can have a wonderful morning and a catastrophic afternoon.

This is not mood instability in the clinical sense. It is a nervous system that is constantly recalibrating in response to demand load. When demands drop, the system settles and the child appears fine. When demands rise (even invisibly, even in ways you cannot see) the system activates and the child appears to become a completely different person. They are not a different person. They are the same person in a different nervous system state.

This variability is one of the most disorienting features for parents because it undermines your ability to predict what is coming. The child who handled the grocery store perfectly last week falls apart in aisle three this week. Nothing was different. Everything was different: sleep was worse, a demand at school depleted the budget, the store was louder, you were carrying tension from a phone call. The demand load was different, even though the setting was the same.

Masking

If your child's school tells you they are "fine" while your home says otherwise, that gap has a name: masking.

Your child is spending enormous energy suppressing their demand avoidance in environments where they do not feel safe enough to show it. School is a high-demand environment: social performance, schedule compliance, sensory input, transitions, instruction-following, sitting still. Your child holds all of that together through sustained effort. They may do it well. They may appear indistinguishable from their peers.

The cost of that suppression is paid at home. The collapse you see after school is not caused by home. It is caused by the accumulated demand load of masking all day. You are seeing the real child. The school is seeing the performance.

This is why the first thirty to sixty minutes after school should be completely demand-free. Their window is likely depleted. They need recovery before anything else is possible. "How was school?" the moment they walk in is a demand. Having a snack available without requiring them to come to the table is not.

If you have ever been told "they're fine at school, the problem must be at home," now you know what is actually happening. The problem is not at home. Home is where they are safe enough to stop performing. That is not a sign that home is the issue. It is a sign that your child trusts home enough to let go.

PDA across ages

The mechanisms do not change with age. What changes is the presentation.

In young children (roughly 3 to 7), demand sensitivity often looks like extreme resistance to basic caregiving routines. Getting dressed, eating, bathing, leaving the house, going to bed. The intensity is what sets it apart from typical toddler and preschool resistance. These are not brief protests. They can last for an hour or more. They are not responsive to the strategies that work for most young children.

In school-age children (roughly 7 to 12), the strategic avoidance becomes more visible. Negotiation, excuse-making, distraction, charm. School refusal or school avoidance often begins in this period as the cumulative demand load of the school day exceeds what the nervous system can hold. The gap between school performance and home behavior widens.

In teenagers (roughly 13 to 17), the developmental push toward independence adds a new layer. The teenager needs autonomy to regulate, but the demands involved in becoming independent (managing schedules, applying for things, navigating social expectations) are themselves activating. School dropout, social withdrawal, gaming as a demand-free zone, and conflict with parents over expectations are common. What adults read as laziness or lack of motivation is a nervous system that has been in chronic overload. Part 5 of this book addresses the teen and young adult years in depth.

In adults, many people discover PDA after their child is identified. Looking back, the pattern was always there. The jobs that were fine until they felt obligatory. The relationships that became suffocating once they carried expectation. The chronic underachievement despite obvious capability.

PDA is not ODD

This misdiagnosis happens frequently and the consequences are serious.

Oppositional Defiant Disorder (ODD) describes a pattern of angry, irritable, argumentative, and defiant behavior. On the surface, PDA can look similar. A child who refuses to comply, who argues, who has explosive reactions to being told what to do.

The mechanisms are completely different. ODD is conceptualized as a behavioral pattern involving anger and hostility toward authority figures. PDA is an anxiety-driven nervous system response to demands as a stimulus class. The ODD child is angry at the person making the demand. The PDA child is overwhelmed by the demand itself, regardless of who is making it. Including demands they place on themselves.

This distinction matters because the standard interventions for ODD (consequences, behavioral contracts, consistent boundaries) are precisely the approaches that make PDA worse. They add demands on top of an already overloaded system. If your child has been diagnosed with ODD and nothing has worked, it is worth asking whether the underlying mechanism is demand sensitivity rather than opposition.

PDA is not just anxiety

PDA involves anxiety. It is driven by anxiety. But it is not the same as generalized anxiety, social anxiety, or specific phobias.

Standard anxiety treatment often focuses on gradual exposure and cognitive restructuring: helping the person tolerate feared situations by building up slowly and reframing the threat. These approaches assume the thinking brain can be engaged to evaluate and update the fear response.

In PDA, the threat response fires subcortically, before the thinking brain is available. Exposure-based approaches can actually make PDA worse, because forcing the person into the demand does not build tolerance. It confirms the threat. The child who is pushed to attend school every day despite severe avoidance does not adapt. The nervous system does not habituate to genuine threat through repetition. It sensitizes.

The anxiety in PDA is also specifically demand-linked. It is not free-floating worry. It is not social fear in general. It is a nervous system response to the specific stimulus of demands: anything that carries an expectation, an obligation, or a requirement. This specificity is what makes PDA-specific approaches necessary.

PDA and autism

PDA is most commonly understood as a profile within autism. Most people identified with PDA are autistic or show significant autistic traits. The diagnostic picture is still evolving, and if your child has PDA features without a formal autism diagnosis, this book still applies.

The PDA features (demand avoidance, social masking, the intense need for control) sit on top of an autistic neurology that includes sensory sensitivities, intense interests, social communication differences, and a need for sameness and predictability. These features interact. Sensory overload narrows the window of tolerance, which makes demands harder to manage. Intense interests provide regulation and safety. Understanding your child as autistic with a PDA profile, rather than as a defiant child or an anxious child, changes what you are looking at.

PDA also rarely exists in isolation. Many children with PDA also have ADHD, anxiety, OCD, sensory processing differences, or trauma histories. These co-occurring conditions interact with demand sensitivity in ways that affect how the framework is applied. A child with both PDA and ADHD may need demand reduction and executive function support simultaneously. A child with PDA and a trauma history may have a nervous system responding to both perceived demands and perceived danger from a different source entirely. This does not make the framework less useful. It makes having a provider who understands the full picture more important.

Your child knows something is different. They have watched themselves refuse things they wanted to do. They have felt the surge of panic when a simple request landed like a threat. They have seen their peers handle things that feel impossible to them. They may not have words for it. But they have the experience.

They are not having a good time either.

PART TWO

We Know What You're Living With

PART TWO

Chapter 4: Your Mornings, Your Evenings, Your Life

It is 7:14 AM. Your child is on the floor. They are not dressed. They are not going to be dressed anytime soon. The bus comes in eleven minutes. You have said "shoes" four times. You have not yelled yet but you can feel it building in your chest, that tight hot thing behind your sternum that means you are about thirty seconds from becoming a person you do not want to be.

Your other child is eating cereal and watching this happen. They have learned to eat fast.

You know you are not supposed to escalate. You read something about that once, or maybe twelve times. You know you are supposed to stay calm, offer choices, lower demands. But the bus comes in eleven minutes and your child is on the floor and the choices you offered ten minutes ago were ignored and the only demand left is "put clothes on your body" and apparently that is too much.

So you pick the clothes up. You put them next to your child. You say something like "the clothes are here when you're ready" in a voice that sounds calm if you do not listen too carefully. Then you walk into the kitchen and grip the counter and breathe through your nose while your other child finishes their cereal in silence.

The bus comes. Your child is not on it. You drive them to school twenty minutes late, in yesterday's shirt, without breakfast, and neither of you speaks in the car.

This is a Tuesday.

The afternoon

They come home from school and the door opens and you can see it in their body before they have said a word. The shoulders. The jaw. The way they drop their bag like it weighs forty pounds. They are done. Whatever capacity they had this morning, the school day used all of it.

You know you are not supposed to ask how school was. You know that question is a demand. You have learned that much. So you do not ask. You put a snack on the counter and you say nothing and you wait.

They go to their room. The door closes. You hear the sound of a screen turning on and you know they will be on it for the next three hours and you are not going to say anything about it because the alternative is another meltdown and you do not have another meltdown in you today.

You stand in the kitchen and eat the snack you made for them.

The evening

Dinner is its own negotiation. They will not come to the table. Or they will come to the table but they will not eat what you made. Or they will eat but only if they can eat on the couch, with their screen, wearing headphones, and you are not allowed to comment on any of it.

You know other families sit at the table together. You have seen them do it. You have memories of imagining you would do it too. That image is from a different life.

Homework does not happen. It has not happened consistently in months. You have received three emails from the teacher this week. You have not responded to any of them yet because you do not know what to say. "My child's nervous system cannot tolerate the demand of homework after six hours of masking at school" is accurate but you are not sure the teacher will hear it the way you mean it.

Bedtime takes an hour and a half. It used to take forty-five minutes. It used to take twenty. You cannot remember when twenty minutes was enough. The routine has fifteen steps and your child can tolerate about three of them on a good night. You have already cut it down twice. The remaining steps are: pajamas, teeth, bed. Somehow those three things still take ninety minutes.

By the time they are asleep you are on the couch and you have nothing left. You are not going to exercise. You are not going to read. You are not going to have a conversation with your partner that is about anything other than what happened today and what needs to happen tomorrow. You are going to sit here until you can convince yourself to go to bed, and then you are going to lie there thinking about whether you are doing this right.

You are not sure you are doing this right. You are not sure anyone is.

The weekend

Weekends are supposed to be easier. There is no school. There is no bus. There is no schedule. And some weekends, it is easier. The demand load drops and your child has room and you see the version of them that you know is in there. They laugh. They play. They let you sit near them. Those moments are real and they keep you going.

Other weekends are worse than the weekdays. Because the structure is gone. Because the day stretches out with no anchors and the formlessness is its own kind of demand. Because you made plans (a birthday party, a family visit, a trip to the store) and the plans became demands and the demands exceeded the budget before you left the driveway.

You cancel the plans. Again. You tell the other family you are sorry. Again. You absorb the disappointment of your other children, who wanted to go and cannot understand why they never get to do anything. You tell them you will try again next weekend. You mean it when you say it. You are not sure you believe it.

The birthday party invitations have stopped coming. You noticed.

The things no one sees

There is a version of your life that is visible to the people around you: the missed school days, the canceled plans, the child who will not come out of their room. People see those things and form opinions. They think you are too soft. They think you need to be firmer. They think your child needs consequences, structure, a different school, a different diet, more fresh air, less screen time, more socialization, less coddling.

They do not see the four hours you spent last night reading about PDA on your phone while your child slept.

They do not see the eleven parenting approaches you have tried in the past two years, each one recommended by someone who was certain it would work, each one failing in the same way and sometimes in new ways.

They do not see you lying in bed calculating whether your child will be able to live independently when they are twenty-five. Or thirty. Or ever.

They do not see the conversation you had with your partner last week where one of you said "I don't know how much longer I can do this" and both of you knew it was true and neither of you had an answer.

They do not see the guilt. The guilt is constant. You feel guilty when you push too hard. You feel guilty when you do not push enough. You feel guilty when you lose your temper. You feel guilty when you accommodate, because somewhere in the back of your mind a voice is telling you that accommodation is the same as giving up. You feel guilty about your other children, who are getting less of you because this child needs so much. You feel guilty about feeling guilty, because your child did not choose this and neither did you and guilt is not helping anyone.

They do not see you Googling "am I a bad parent" at 1 AM. More than once.

You are not a bad parent. You have been parenting hard, with the wrong tools, for a long time. The tools were not wrong because you chose badly. They were wrong because they were designed for a different nervous system. You did not know that. Nobody told you.

What you have tried

You have tried reward charts. They worked for three days. Then they became a demand and your child stopped responding to them. You tried making the rewards bigger. That worked for two days. Then it stopped too.

You have tried consequences. Natural consequences, logical consequences, the consequence of losing a privilege. Your child either did not care (because the avoidance was stronger than the desire for the privilege) or they cared enormously and the consequence produced a meltdown so severe that the original demand was forgotten entirely.

You have tried gentle parenting. You validated feelings. You offered choices. You got down on their level and made eye contact and used a calm voice. It helped sometimes. It did not help when their window was closed, because when the window is closed, your calm voice is still arriving at a nervous system that has already activated. The words do not matter when the system is in survival mode.

You have tried being firmer. You drew a line. You held it. Your child escalated past the line into territory that scared both of you. You held the line anyway because someone told you that consistency was the key. Consistency made it worse. Not because consistency is bad advice in general. Because consistent application of an approach that activates the nervous system consistently activates the nervous system. The line was the problem, not your ability to hold it.

You have tried therapy. Your child's therapist was kind. They used strategies designed for anxious children or oppositional children. The strategies assumed your child could access their thinking brain during the difficult moments. Your child could not. The therapy did not fail because the therapist was bad. It failed because the model did not account for what was actually happening.

None of this was your fault. None of it was wasted. Every approach you tried taught you something about what does not work for your child's nervous system. That information matters. It is part of the picture you are building.

PART TWO

Chapter 5: You Are Still the Parent

If you have read this far, you are probably already wondering something that feels dangerous to say out loud.

If I lower demands, stop using consequences, and let my child's nervous system lead, am I still parenting?

Yes. You are.

But what parenting looks like is about to change. That change will be uncomfortable. Not because it is wrong. Because it does not match what you were taught parenting is supposed to be.

The old engine

Most of what you learned about raising children runs on one mechanism: external pressure produces desired behavior. Set the expectation. Enforce the boundary. Apply the consequence. The child learns because the cost of not learning is high enough.

That engine works for most children. It does not work for yours. Not because you are doing it wrong. Because external pressure is the thing their nervous system reads as threat. The engine most parents rely on is the engine that makes your child's system shut down.

You have already experienced this. You set an expectation. You enforced it consistently. Your child escalated. You held firm. They escalated past the point where holding firm made sense. The interaction ended with both of you worse off than when it started. You tried again the next day because someone told you consistency was the answer. Consistency did not produce compliance. It produced sensitization. The nervous system did not habituate to the demand through repetition. It learned to detect it faster and respond harder.

This is not a failure of your consistency. It is a predictable outcome of applying consistent pressure to a nervous system that processes pressure as threat.

The new engine

RELATE replaces the engine. It does not replace parenting.

You are still teaching your child. You are still holding expectations. You are still building the skills they will need to function in a world that will not lower demands for them. The difference is how you get there.

Instead of compliance driven by pressure, you are building capacity driven by safety. Your child cooperates because their nervous system is regulated enough to handle what you are asking. Not because they fear the consequence. Because they have the capacity. That distinction sounds abstract right now. It will become concrete in Part 3 when you see the framework applied to your actual mornings, your actual bedtimes, your actual life. For now, the principle: safety produces capacity. Pressure depletes it.

The question that changes everything

Every time you encounter resistance from your child, you have a decision to make. The decision is not "should I lower this demand?" That framing will collapse you because the answer starts to feel like it is always yes and then you are not parenting at all.

The question is simpler.

Is my child's window open or closed right now?

That is it. Everything follows from the answer.

The window of tolerance is the zone of nervous system arousal within which your child can think flexibly, manage discomfort, cooperate with you, and handle the demands of the moment. When the window is open, these capacities are available. When the window is closed, they are not available. Not withheld. Not being stubborn about. Genuinely unavailable, the same way you cannot read a book while someone is screaming in your ear. The capacity is offline.

If their window is open: parent. Hold the expectation. A child who does not want to brush their teeth but can is having a normal human moment. Not a PDA moment. You can hold that line. You can say "I know you don't want to, and it's time." The demand does not need lowering. You are parenting a child who would rather not, and every child would rather not sometimes.

If their window is closed: holding the expectation is not parenting. It is stacking demands on a system that has nothing left. Lower the demand. Wait. Revisit when the window opens. This is not permissiveness. It is accurate load management. A physical therapist does not load a recovering knee with the pre-injury weight and call it "consistency." They assess current capacity and load accordingly. You are doing the same thing with demand load.

If you are not sure (and you often will not be sure, that is honest and that is okay): try the smallest version of the demand. Not the full expectation and not nothing. Something in between. "Can you get your shoes near the door?" instead of "get your shoes on, we need to go." Their response to the smaller ask will tell you where they are. If they can handle it, try the next step. If they cannot, you have your answer.

This is not a flowchart you memorize. It is a habit you build. Over time, reading the window becomes automatic. You will learn your child's specific signals: the posture shift that means the window is narrowing, the vocal tone that means it is closed, the body language that means there is room. Chapter 7 teaches you how to read those signals in detail.

What you are not doing

You are not giving up expectations. You are timing them to capacity.

You are not letting your child do whatever they want. You are recognizing that a demand placed on a closed window does not produce compliance. It produces crisis. And crisis costs more than the accommodation would have.

You are not avoiding the hard things. You are creating the conditions under which the hard things become possible. A child whose demand budget has room in it can tolerate a demand they do not like. A child whose demand budget is overdrawn cannot tolerate anything.

You are not being permissive. Permissive parenting means no expectations. This is not that. This is accurate parenting: matching what you ask to what the nervous system can hold right now, and building the capacity to hold more over time.

What traditional advice gets wrong

You will hear things from well-meaning people that sound like common sense and are exactly wrong for your child. You have probably already heard most of them.

"They need consistent boundaries." Consistency is good advice when the approach is sound. Consistently applying approaches that activate the nervous system consistently activates the nervous system. The nervous system does not habituate to genuine threat through repetition. It sensitizes.

"They need to learn they can't always get what they want." This assumes the behavior is a learning problem. It is a nervous system problem. You cannot learn your way out of a flinch.

"You're reinforcing the behavior by giving in." Reinforcement assumes a cost-benefit calculation. The threat response is not a calculation. It is a reflex. You cannot reinforce or extinguish a reflex through consequences. You change what triggers it.

"If you keep lowering demands, they'll never learn to handle them." Capacity does not build through exposure to demands the system cannot handle. It builds through sustained safety, reduced demand load, and gradual reintroduction at the edges of the window. That is what this framework does.

These assessments are not coming from bad people. They are coming from people applying a neurotypical framework to a situation it does not fit. The advice is right for most children and wrong for yours. Knowing that does not make it easier to hear. But it does make it easier to discard.

The line between accommodation and abdication

There is a real question buried underneath the anxiety about whether you are still parenting. The question is: where is the line?

The line is the window.

When the window is open and your child resists a demand, you hold it. You hold it warmly, without escalation, without threat, but you hold it. "I know this is hard. It's time to brush your teeth." That is parenting. That is appropriate. That is what a regulated child with a demand sensitive nervous system can handle when their window is open.

When the window is closed and your child resists a demand, you release it. Not because you are giving up. Because holding a demand on a closed window does not produce the outcome you want. It produces damage to the relationship, depletion of the demand budget, and sensitization of the threat response. The demand you forced today made tomorrow's demand harder. The math does not work.

The skill you are building is not "lower all demands." It is "read the window accurately and respond accordingly." Some days you will hold more demands than you expect. Some days you will hold almost none. Both of those days are parenting. The quality of your parenting is not measured by the number of demands you enforce. It is measured by the accuracy of your response to your child's nervous system state.

That is a harder standard than the old one. "Be consistent" is simple. "Read the window in real time and adjust on the fly" is complex. But it is the standard that works for this nervous system. And you are already better at it than you think. You have been reading your child's state for years. You just did not have the framework to act on what you were seeing.

PART TWO

Chapter 6: The Picture Is Gone

You had a picture of what raising this child would look like.

Maybe it was specific. Birthday parties with friends. Homework at the kitchen table while you made dinner. Bedtime routines that ended with a story and a kiss and a "goodnight, I love you" that your child said back without prompting. Family vacations where everyone was mostly happy. Soccer games or dance recitals or school plays where your child participated in something and you sat in the audience and felt the thing parents are supposed to feel.

Maybe it was vague. Just an assumption that things would be hard sometimes but mostly navigable. That the hard parts would be the normal hard parts: a bad grade, a fight with a friend, the time they lied about something and you had to have that conversation. The hard parts that other parents complain about. The hard parts you would welcome right now because at least they would be recognizable.

That picture is gone. Not temporarily misplaced. Not waiting for the right intervention to bring it back. Gone.

You are allowed to grieve it.

Why this matters

This is not a detour from the practical content of this book. It is connected to it directly.

Unnamed grief turns into resentment. Resentment leaks. It leaks into your tone when you are tired. It leaks into the way you sigh when your child refuses something for the third time in an hour. It leaks into the distance between what you are saying and what your face is communicating. Your child's nervous system reads the leak. It does not know what it is reading. It just registers that something in you is off, and it adjusts its own threat level accordingly.

Grief that has been acknowledged, sat with, and allowed to exist does not leak the same way. It is still there. It does not go away. But it stops running the show from underneath.

So this chapter is not about moving past the grief. It is about naming it clearly enough that it stops operating in the background of every interaction.

What you are grieving

You are grieving the ease. Other families move through their days with a kind of friction that is manageable. Getting out the door takes ten minutes, not ninety. Bedtime is a process, not a siege. The family can go to a restaurant and mostly enjoy it. You see these families at the grocery store and in the school parking lot and on social media and the gap between their daily life and yours feels unbridgeable.

You are grieving the relationship you imagined. You expected to have a child who would run to you when you picked them up from school. Who would crawl into your lap with a book. Who would say "I love you" without being prompted and mean it in a way you could feel. What you have, some days, is a child who cannot tolerate your proximity. Who flinches when you reach for them. Who seems to prefer being alone to being with you. The rejection is not real (it is self-protection, not rejection, and Chapter 7 explains the difference) but it feels real. It feels real every single day.

You are grieving the milestones. The ones that happened differently and the ones that have not happened at all. The birthday party they could not attend. The sport they could not sustain. The school trip they could not go on. The friendships that did not form because the social demand load was too high. You watch other children move through the developmental sequence and your child is not on that sequence and no one can tell you what their sequence looks like.

You are grieving your own life. The career you adjusted or abandoned. The friendships that required reciprocity you no longer had the capacity for. The hobbies that needed time the crisis absorbed. The marriage or partnership that needed your presence and got whatever was left after the PDA consumed the rest. You have become, in ways you did not choose, a person whose primary identity is managing a crisis. That is not who you planned to be.

You are grieving the future you assumed. The independence. The college. The job. The apartment. The grandchildren. Some version of your child moving through the world in a way that did not require you to manage it. You do not know what the future looks like now. Nobody can tell you, because the research is not there yet and the outcomes are not documented and the honest answer is: it depends on a lot of things, and some of those things have not happened yet.

That uncertainty is its own grief. You cannot mourn a specific loss because you do not know what the loss is. You are grieving a blank space where a picture used to be.

What the grief is not

The grief is not a sign that you have not accepted your child. You can love your child completely, fiercely, without reservation, and still mourn the family life you expected. Both things are true. Both things are allowed. Anyone who tells you that grieving the picture means you do not love the reality is wrong. They are confusing acceptance with the absence of loss. Acceptance and loss coexist. They will coexist for a long time, possibly forever, and that is not a problem to solve.

The grief is not a sign that you are failing at this. It is a sign that you are human and the distance between what you imagined and what is real is significant. Pretending the distance is not there does not make you a better parent. It makes you a parent who is carrying unacknowledged weight, and that weight shows up in your nervous system, which shows up in your child's environment.

The grief is not something you process once and finish. It comes back. It comes back when you see a family doing something yours cannot do. It comes back at milestones. It comes back at 2 AM for no identifiable reason. Each time it comes back, you do not need to process it from the beginning. You just need to let it be there without pretending it is not.

What to do with it

Name it. To yourself, out loud if you can. "I am grieving the parenting experience I expected and the family life I imagined." That sentence, said honestly, reduces the power of the grief to operate beneath your awareness.

Share it with someone who can hold it. Not someone who will try to fix it. Not someone who will say "but your child is such a gift" or "everything happens for a reason" or "have you tried." Someone who will listen and not flinch and not redirect you to gratitude. If you do not have that person, finding them is not a luxury. It is infrastructure. Chapter 13 talks about what you actually need in terms of support, and this is one of the things you need.

Do not perform resolution you do not feel. You do not need to "make peace with it" on anyone's timeline, including your own. You do not need to find the silver lining. You do not need to frame your child's disability as a gift that taught you something. It may be all of those things eventually. It does not have to be any of them right now.

What you are building instead

The picture is gone. What you are building in its place is not lesser. It is different. It is real. It is yours.

The version of connection you build with a demand sensitive child does not look like the parenting magazine version. It looks like sitting on the couch in silence while your child plays on the floor nearby and neither of you speaks and both of you are okay. It looks like a meme texted from the next room. It looks like the moment, three months into doing this differently, when your child sits one cushion closer than they used to and neither of you mentions it.

The version of progress you see is not dramatic. It is a meltdown that lasted twenty minutes instead of forty-five. It is a morning that needed two prompts instead of seven. It is your child tolerating something they could not tolerate last month. It is a repair that happened in an hour instead of a day.

These are not lesser milestones. They are the milestones that belong to your family. They are real and they are hard-won and they count.

PART THREE

The RELATE Framework at Home

PART THREE

Chapter 7: How Connection Works

Connection with a demand sensitive child does not look like what you expected. It does not look like what the books describe. It does not look like what you see other families doing. It looks like something quieter, stranger, and harder to trust.

It looks like sitting in the same room while your child ignores you. It looks like watching their game without commenting on it. It looks like a snack placed on the counter without a word. It looks like the moment, weeks into this, when they sit one cushion closer than they used to and neither of you mentions it.

If that does not sound like connection, this chapter will change your mind. Because the reason those moments work is not sentimental. It is neurological. And understanding the neurology changes what you do, what you stop doing, and how you read what your child is telling you without words.

Co-regulation: the mechanism underneath everything

Before we talk about how to connect, you need to understand why your presence matters at the level of the nervous system. This is not a side note. This is the mechanism that makes the entire framework function.

Co-regulation is the process by which one nervous system influences another. It is not a technique you learn. It is a biological process that operates constantly, below conscious awareness, in both directions. Your nervous system and your child's nervous system are in continuous communication through channels that are faster than language: facial expression, muscle tension, vocal pitch, breathing rate, posture, the pace of your movements, the quality of your attention, the tension in your hands, the set of your jaw.

Your child's nervous system is reading yours right now. Not your words. Not your intentions. Your body. If you are holding this book and feeling anxious about what you are going to learn, your body is transmitting that anxiety through micro-signals you are not aware of producing. If you are calm and curious, your body is transmitting that instead.

This is happening all the time, in both directions, whether anyone is trying to make it happen or not.

Here is what co-regulation looks like in practice.

You walk into the room where your child is playing. You have just had a stressful phone call. You have not said a word about it. You are smiling. You ask casually if they want a snack. Your child tenses. They do not answer. They pull slightly away from you, or they get irritable, or they say "go away" with a sharpness that seems to come from nowhere. You did not do anything wrong. You asked about a snack. But your nervous system was carrying the residue of the phone call, and their system read it. It did not read the smile or the casual tone. It read the activation underneath, and it responded to the truth, not the performance.

Now a different version. You have had the same phone call. But before you walk into the room, you take sixty seconds. You breathe. You unclench your jaw. You notice the tension in your shoulders and let it drop. You walk in and you do not say anything at all. You sit down on the other end of the couch. You pick up a magazine or your phone. You are not performing. You are just present, and your body has settled enough that what you are transmitting is closer to neutral. Your child does not tense. They keep playing. Five minutes later they say something about their game, not to you exactly, but out loud, knowing you can hear.

Same parent. Same child. Same room. Different nervous system state walking in the door. Different outcome. That is co-regulation.

This works in both directions. When your child is activated, your nervous system feels the pull. Your heart rate rises. Your jaw tightens. Your voice gets a little higher, a little faster. You start transmitting urgency, which their system reads as additional threat, which increases their activation, which increases yours. Two tuning forks vibrating each other higher. Two nervous systems pulling each other further from the window.

When you are regulated and your child is activated, something different can happen. Your steady state becomes a signal. Not a demand. Not a command to calm down. A signal that the environment contains something safe. Their nervous system, which is scanning constantly for threat and safety cues, encounters your regulation and has the option of matching it. Not immediately. Not reliably. Not every time. But over minutes, sometimes over hours, a regulated parent in the room changes what the child's nervous system encounters. And what it encounters is what determines what it does.

This is why "calm down" does not work but your calm does. The words are a demand. Your state is information. Their nervous system does not process your instruction to regulate. It processes your regulation itself, and responds to that. The words are noise. The nervous system state is signal.

This is also why you cannot fake it. If you are performing calm while your internal state is activated, the performance is a mismatch. Your words say one thing. Your breathing rate, your muscle tension, your vocal pitch say another. Your child's nervous system reads the mismatch and responds to the truth underneath, not the performance on top. They are not being difficult when they do this. They are not being defiant or perceptive or manipulative. Their threat-detection system is doing exactly what it evolved to do: reading the actual state of the people around them, not the stated state. Performing calm while activated internally is like putting a "friendly dog" sign on a fence while the dog behind it is growling. The sign is not the relevant information.

What does this mean practically? It means the single most impactful thing you can do before any interaction with your child is check your own state. Not to be perfect. Not to always be calm. That is not realistic and asking it of yourself is another demand on a system that already has too many. But to notice. Am I activated right now? Is my jaw tight? Am I holding my breath? Am I carrying something from the last hour that has nothing to do with my child?

If you are, and you have thirty seconds, use them. Breathe. Unclench. Slow down. Not because you owe your child a perfect nervous system. Because the physics of co-regulation mean that whatever state you walk in with is the state their system will encounter first, and that encounter shapes everything that follows.

We will come back to your regulation in depth in Part 4. For now, the point is this: connection with your child is not primarily about what you say or what you do. It is about what your nervous system is broadcasting while you say and do it. A parent who is genuinely settled and present, doing nothing, is providing more co-regulation than a parent who is anxious and performing a bonding activity. Presence without agenda from a regulated nervous system. That is the foundation.

The account balance

Think of the relationship between you and your child as a bank account. Every demand is a withdrawal. Getting dressed. Brushing teeth. Leaving the house. Homework. Transitions. Corrections. Questions. Time pressure. Social expectations. "How was your day?" A raised eyebrow when they reach for the screen. The sigh you did not mean to let out. Each one takes something out.

Every non-contingent connection is a deposit. Your calm presence with no agenda. Following their lead in play. A snack placed without comment. Shared silence. Sitting near them without wanting anything from them.

The word "non-contingent" is doing important work. It means the connection is not attached to a condition. "I will spend time with you if you get dressed first" is not a deposit. It is a transaction. "I will sit with you because I want to be near you" is a deposit, but only if it is true, and only if your child does not owe you anything in return. Not a response. Not a thank you. Not engagement. Not acknowledgment that you are there. The deposit has to be free. No strings. No hidden expectation. No agenda underneath. The moment an agenda attaches, the deposit becomes a demand, and the account gets a withdrawal instead.

If you are making ten withdrawals a day and one deposit, the account is overdrawn. Everything in this framework becomes harder from an overdrawn account. ADAPT from Chapter 9 works less well when the child does not trust the relationship enough to let you co-regulate. The pillars in Chapter 8 work less well when there is no relational foundation underneath them. Repair from Chapter 15 takes longer and lands less cleanly when the account has been running a deficit for months.

The good news: deposits are small and free. Five minutes of sitting near them without an agenda. Three minutes of watching their game without commentary. A plate of food left on the counter without words. A drive with their music playing and your mouth closed. These are not time-intensive interventions. They are small, repeatable, daily investments. They compound.

One intentional moment of low-demand connection per day changes the trajectory over weeks. Not because one moment is transformative. Because the nervous system tracks patterns. A parent who shows up without agenda, consistently, over time, deposits evidence into the child's nervous system that this relationship is not a source of threat. That evidence accumulates. It cannot be rushed. It cannot be manufactured in a weekend of intensive bonding. It builds slowly, through repetition, the same way trust builds in any relationship. Except this one requires you to keep depositing without receiving much back for a while. That is hard. That is real. That is the work.

The five modes of low-demand connection

These are not activities to schedule. They are not a program. They are ways of showing up. Each one carries a different demand load. Start with the lowest and let your child's nervous system tell you when it can tolerate more.

1. Be Near

Parallel presence. You are in the same room, doing your own thing. Available but not seeking. You are not watching them. You are not waiting for a moment to engage. You are simply present, with no agenda.

This is the baseline everything else is built on. Most parents skip it because it does not feel like bonding. It does not look like connection. Nothing is happening. You are sitting on the couch reading while they play on the floor. You are cooking while they sit at the counter on their tablet. You are folding laundry in the room where they are drawing. No conversation required. No eye contact. Just shared space.

For a nervous system that experiences most human proximity as a demand, a person who is near and wants nothing is profoundly regulating. Think about what your child encounters from most people. Teachers want them to perform. Relatives want them to be social. Peers want them to follow the rules of the game. Therapists want them to talk about their feelings. Almost every person in their life arrives with an agenda attached. You, sitting in the same room and wanting nothing, are the exception. That exception is the safest form of closeness that exists for many demand sensitive children. A person who is near and wants nothing. That is the complete action.

Do not use Be Near as a setup to eventually engage. They will feel the agenda. If you are sitting near them and internally waiting for the right moment to start a conversation, you are not doing Be Near. You are doing surveillance with a patient face. Their nervous system knows the difference. Your posture knows the difference. The quality of your attention knows the difference.

Say nothing. Do your own thing. Be available if they come to you. Do not go to them. Not today. Not yet. Just be near.

2. Follow In

Enter their world on their terms. They are playing a game. Sit and watch without commentary. They are building something. Watch, or build your own nearby. They are talking about their intense interest. Listen without redirecting, without teaching, without connecting it to something "useful."

You are a guest in their world. They set the terms.

The neurological shift here is significant. In most parent-child interactions, the parent sets the activity, the pace, and the rules. That is how playtime works in most families. The parent suggests the game, facilitates the turn-taking, makes sure it is educational or enriching or at least not pure screen time. Following In reverses that completely. The child is in control. The autonomy-threat mechanism quiets because there is no constraint on their choice. The Intolerance of Uncertainty mechanism quiets because they are the one determining what happens next. You are not an unknown variable. You are a follower.

What it looks like: they are watching YouTube videos about their interest. You sit nearby and watch too. Not with a look on your face that says "I am trying to bond with you by enduring this." With genuine attention. If you cannot actually become interested, that is fine. Sit nearby and let them see that you are present while they do their thing. They are playing Minecraft. You ask "can I watch?" once. Then you actually watch. Without suggesting they build something different. Without asking what the goal is. Without offering to play together. You asked to watch. Watch. They are sorting their collection of rocks or figurines or cards. You sit nearby and let them narrate or not, without asking questions. Without saying "oh, what's that one?" unless they have invited questions through their body language.

Do not turn Follow In into a teachable moment. The instant you say "that's interesting, did you know that in real life..." you have left their world and pulled them into yours. The instant you suggest an improvement to their build, you have added a demand. The instant you redirect their interest toward something more productive, you have communicated that their world is not enough. Follow means follow. It does not mean follow and then steer.

The temptation to teach, improve, or redirect is strong. It comes from a good place. You want to connect through their interest and you know things about the topic and sharing knowledge is how adults show engagement. Resist it. The connection is in your presence, not your contribution. Later, when the relational account has more in it, there will be room for you to bring more of yourself. For now, follow.

3. Be Used

"Hold this." "Be the bad guy." "Watch me do this." "You're the customer and I'm the shop owner." "Stand there and don't move." "Say this exact sentence."

These are connection bids from your child. They look nothing like what most parents expect. They look like bossiness. They feel like being ordered around. They can be exhausting, repetitive, and strange. Your child assigns you a role, dictates the terms, directs every detail, and becomes upset if you deviate from the script they have in their head.

This is one of the most powerful connection modes available for demand sensitive children, and it is one of the most commonly missed. When your child directs you, assigns you a role, or tells you what to do in their play, they are choosing to include you. That is significant. They are building an interaction in which they have complete control over the terms. The autonomy mechanism is quiet because they are in charge. The uncertainty mechanism is quiet because they are writing the script. The threat detection mechanism is quiet because nothing is being asked of them. The only person being asked to do something is you.

Your job is to comply without improving, correcting, or expanding. If they say "you're the customer," be the customer. Do not add a subplot. Do not make the game more educational. Do not suggest taking turns being the shop owner. Do not redirect toward a version of the game that involves more turn-taking or social skills practice. Play the role they gave you, the way they gave it to you, for as long as they want, without commentary on the process.

Parents often experience being directed this way as rude, inflexible, or controlling. Reframe it: your child is solving the connection problem. They want to be with you but cannot tolerate the demand load of typical interaction. They have found a format in which connection is possible because they hold all the control. That is not a deficit. That is creative problem-solving by a nervous system that needs different conditions for connection than most people require.

Accept it exactly as offered. The relationship deposits from thirty minutes of being bossed around in their imaginary restaurant are larger than you think.

4. Offer Without Requiring

Low-demand bids from you. A snack placed nearby without comment. "I'm watching something if you want to join." A link to something related to their interest, texted with no follow-up. Their favorite blanket moved to the couch without mentioning it. Something they like, left where they will find it.

The key distinction: every offer must have a genuine "no" available. If you will be hurt by rejection, disappointed by no response, or frustrated if they ignore it, it is not an offer. It is a demand wearing generosity's clothing. Your child's nervous system will detect the expectation underneath. It always does. Always.

What a genuine offer looks like: you make their favorite snack and put it on the counter. You do not say "I made this for you." You do not look to see if they notice. You do not bring it up later. It is on the counter. If they eat it, good. If they do not, good. No data was generated about the relationship either way. The offer was complete when you set it down.

You mention you are going on a walk and they are welcome to come. The period at the end of that sentence is real. They say no. You go on the walk. You do not come back and say "you missed a nice walk." You do not look disappointed. You do not alter your tone for the rest of the evening. The offer had a genuine no. The no was used. The interaction is over.

You text them a meme related to their interest. They do not respond. You do not follow up. You do not say "did you see what I sent you?" You do not feel rejected. The meme was an offer, not an opening bid in a conversation they are now obligated to continue.

What a non-genuine offer looks like: "I made you a snack, don't you want it?" That is a demand. "I'm going for a walk, it would be really nice if you came." That is a guilt-wrapped demand. "I texted you something, did you see it?" That is a demand for acknowledgment.

The difference between a genuine offer and a demand is not in the words. It is in what happens when they say no. If you are fine with no, it was an offer. If no produces a reaction in you (disappointment, frustration, hurt, withdrawal) it was a demand. Learning to make genuine offers is one of the harder skills in this framework because it requires you to separate your need for reciprocity from the act of giving. Your need for reciprocity is real and valid. But attaching it to the offer turns the offer into a transaction, and your child's nervous system will detect the transaction every time.

5. Shared Rhythm

Activities that connect through physical rhythm rather than verbal exchange. Driving in the car. Walking side by side. Swinging on adjacent swings. Cooking in the same kitchen. Bouncing a ball back and forth. Listening to music together. Rocking in adjacent chairs on the porch. Swimming laps in the same pool.

These work because the connection is in the shared movement and proximity, not in conversation. Eye contact is optional. Silence is welcome. The nervous systems synchronize through rhythm, not words. The co-regulation is happening through a channel that bypasses all of the demand-laden features of typical interaction: no eye contact required, no social performance, no conversation to track, no appropriate responses to generate. Just two bodies in motion, together.

Many parents report that their deepest conversations happen in the car. There is a neurological reason for that. Side by side. Eyes forward. Shared motion. The hum of the engine as a constant background. No demand for face-to-face engagement. The social demand of the interaction is as low as it can get while still being together, and in that low-demand space, things come out. Not always. Not on command. But the car is where many demand sensitive children say the things they cannot say anywhere else, because the setup removes every demand except proximity.

What it looks like: a drive with their music playing. A walk where nobody has to talk. Cooking dinner where they stir and you chop, or they sit on the counter while you cook. Side-by-side gaming, each on your own screen. Walking the dog together in silence. Swinging at the park while they are on the next swing and neither of you is talking.

These do not require planning. They do not require scheduling. They happen inside the routines you already have. The drive to school. The walk to the mailbox. The ten minutes of cooking before dinner. You are already doing shared rhythm without naming it. Name it. Notice when it happens. Do more of it on purpose.

Reading your child's signals

You may be waiting for the connection signals you expected. Eye contact. A hug. An "I love you." An initiated conversation. A request to spend time together. Those may come eventually. They may not come for a long time. In the meantime, your child is sending you signals that look nothing like what you were waiting for.

Connection signals from a demand sensitive child can include: leaving their door open when you are nearby. Narrating their game out loud, not to you, but knowing you can hear. Sitting one cushion closer than they did last month. Showing you something on their screen without being asked. Texting you a meme or a link. Asking for a specific food. Tolerating your presence during a preferred activity. Choosing to be in the same room when they could be in a different one. Making a comment about something you are doing, not a conversation, just a comment. Laughing at something near you when they could have laughed alone.

Each of these is a bid from a nervous system that cannot tolerate direct connection but is reaching toward you indirectly. These bids are easy to miss because they do not look like the bids you were trained to expect. And they are easy to kill.

If you respond with the intensity of your relief ("Oh I love that you're showing me! Tell me more! What else are you working on?") you will overwhelm the bid and teach them that sharing leads to a flood of demands. They showed you something casually. It was a low-energy bid. If you respond with high energy, the cost of sharing just went up, and the next bid will take longer to come.

Instead: match the energy of their bid, not the energy of your need. They showed you something on their screen. "Cool." A nod. A brief smile. Then let it go. They narrated their game out loud. You do not respond at all, or you say "nice" without looking up. They sat one cushion closer. You say nothing. You change nothing. You let the proximity exist without commenting on it.

The next bid will come sooner when the first one was received without intensity. Over weeks, the bids get bigger. Not because you are training them. Because the evidence is accumulating in their nervous system: sharing is safe here. Proximity is safe here. This person receives my bids without turning them into demands.

Safety signals are different from connection signals. Connection signals are bids your child makes toward you. Safety signals are physiological indicators that the nervous system has detected safety. They are not deliberate behaviors. They are automatic.

You can observe them: shoulders dropping, jaw relaxing, hands unclenching. Breathing that deepens and slows. Willingness to make eye contact, if eye contact is something they can do. Physically moving closer without being asked. Voluntarily initiating conversation. Humor appearing. Asking for help or admitting difficulty. A change in vocal tone from flat or tight to more relaxed.

When you see these signals, do not comment on them. "Oh good, you're relaxing!" is a demand. It requires them to be aware of their own state, to agree with your assessment of it, and to maintain the state now that it has been noticed. That sequence can reverse the signal entirely. The safety the nervous system just detected gets replaced by the threat of being observed and evaluated.

Instead: notice. Adjust your approach accordingly. If you are in the middle of an interaction and you see shoulders drop, something you are doing (or stopped doing) just registered as safe. File it. Use it next time. These signals are your real-time data. Over time, reading them becomes more accurate and more automatic. They will tell you more about your child's nervous system state than their words will. More than their compliance will. More than their reported feelings will. The body does not perform. It responds.

What gets in the way

Four things reliably interfere with connection for parents of demand sensitive children.

Parent grief. Chapter 6 named it. You imagined a relationship with your child that included easy affection, shared activities, family outings, bedtime stories. What you got is different. The grief is real and it is allowed. It becomes a problem for connection when it drives you to seek the version of connection your child cannot provide, and the seeking becomes a demand they can feel. You reach for a hug. They pull away. You suggest a game. They refuse. You try to create a moment and it falls apart. The grief underneath those attempts is what the child's nervous system reads. Not the attempt itself, but the wanting underneath it. That wanting is a demand, and it adds to the load.

Feeling rejected. When your child walks away from your bid, ignores your offering, or tells you to leave, it hurts. That hurt is real. But rejection and self-protection look identical from the outside. Your child is not rejecting you. They are protecting a nervous system that cannot tolerate the demand your proximity carries right now. Tomorrow they may tolerate it. Next week they may want it. Right now they cannot, and their "go away" is not about you. It is about the demand budget being empty. The difference matters because if you read it as rejection, you withdraw. You stop offering. You protect yourself. If you read it as self-protection, you stay available without pursuing. You maintain Be Near without pushing for more. Staying available in the face of apparent rejection is one of the hardest things this framework asks of you. It requires separating your emotional experience (real, valid, painful) from the data about your child's nervous system (their response is protective, not personal). Both can be true at the same time.

The instinct to engineer. If you have read this far, you are a problem-solver. You want to schedule connection time, create bonding activities, design a system for increasing relational deposits. You want a plan. Connection with a demand sensitive child resists planning. The moment it becomes a scheduled obligation, it becomes a demand. "Wednesday is our special time" is a demand. The child's nervous system now has to tolerate an expectation, and the expectation is attached to something that is supposed to feel good, which makes the demand harder, not easier. Instead of engineering connection, create the conditions for it. Be Near consistently. Follow In when the opportunity appears. Offer Without Requiring regularly. Let connection emerge from the conditions you have created, on their timeline, in whatever form their nervous system can hold.

Comparing. The family down the street plays board games together. Your sister's kids run to greet her. The Instagram parent is doing a craft project with their smiling child. Your version of connection is sitting in the same room in silence while your child ignores you. That is not less than. It is the version of connection your child's nervous system can hold right now. Comparing your connection to neurotypical connection is using the wrong ruler. It will always come up short, and the feeling of falling short will drive you to push for more, which adds demand, which makes connection harder. Your ruler is: are there more deposits today than there were last month? Is my child tolerating my presence more than they were? Are the bids coming, even small ones? Those are the metrics that matter.

One deposit a day

You do not need all five modes working every day. You do not need any of them every day. But if most days have zero deposits, the account is not getting what it needs.

One intentional moment of low-demand connection per day. Five minutes of Be Near. Three minutes of watching their game. A snack placed without comment. A drive with their music on. That is enough to start.

The deposits compound. The nervous system tracks the pattern. Over weeks, the evidence builds: this person is safe. This relationship is not a threat. That evidence is the foundation the rest of the framework depends on. The six pillars of RELATE work because they are delivered inside a relationship the child's nervous system has learned to trust. Without that trust, the strategies are techniques being applied to a resistant system. With it, they are a framework operating inside a safe relationship.

That distinction is the difference between RELATE working and RELATE not working.

PART THREE

Chapter 8: The Six Pillars in Your House

RELATE is six pillars. Not six independent modules you pick from like a menu. Six dimensions of a single approach, each making the others possible. Relationship without Lower Demands is warmth that still overwhelms. Lower Demands without Empathy feels like you have given up on them. Time without Adjust is patience aimed at the wrong thing. Environment without Relationship is engineering without connection.

You do not need to implement all six perfectly starting tomorrow. You need to understand what they are, how they work together, and where to start.

If you are overwhelmed by six, start with two: Relationship first, Lower Demands second. Those two produce the most immediate change in most families. The others build on what those two establish.

Two things before we go through them. First, Chapter 7 covered connection and co-regulation in depth. The Relationship pillar here will be brief because you already have it. Second, every pillar in this chapter includes specific language. What to say. What not to say. What the demand sensitive version of this looks like in your actual house on a Tuesday. The framework is not conceptual. It is practical. If you cannot use it tomorrow morning, it is not useful.

R: Relationship

Core concept: connection without agenda.

This is the first pillar because everything else depends on it. Chapter 7 teaches the five modes of low-demand connection in detail. The principle is simple: every non-contingent connection is a deposit. Every demand is a withdrawal. If the account is overdrawn, nothing else in this framework works as well as it should.

Start with one intentional deposit per day. Be Near. Follow In. A snack without comment. That is enough for now.

Your child comes downstairs looking tense. Instead of "Good morning! Did you sleep okay? What do you want for breakfast? Don't forget you have that thing at school today," you say: "Morning." And then you are just there. Making coffee. Present. Not performing. Not needing anything from them.

That is Relationship.

E: Empathy

Core concept: seeing the world through their nervous system, not yours.

Empathy in RELATE is not a script you perform. It is not a thing you say to get your child to cooperate. It is a genuine shift in your perspective that changes your internal state. When you actually take your child's perspective, when you feel in your own body what it might be like to experience "put your shoes on" as a genuine threat, something shifts. Your urgency decreases. Your frustration softens. Your jaw unclenches. Your nervous system settles, even slightly.

That shift in your state is what your child's nervous system detects as safety. They are not reading your empathic words. They are reading the state underneath the words. The words are the delivery vehicle. The state is the message. If you say empathic words while internally thinking "we still need to get moving," they will detect the urgency underneath. The words land on a nervous system that has already read the truth. And the truth is what it responds to.

This is why empathy in RELATE is described as perspective-taking that leads to compassion, which leads to a shift in your state, which the child's system detects as safety. It is a chain. You cannot skip to the end. You cannot say empathic words from an unshifted state and expect them to land. Your child's threat-detection system is too accurate for that.

What empathy sounds like when it lands:

What to say	Why it works
"This morning feels really hard."	*Accurate naming. No "but." No solution. Then wait.*
"You don't want to go. I can see that."	*Acknowledges their experience as real. No pivot to why they should.*
"Something about this is really overwhelming right now."	*Said while sitting down. Your body matches your words: no pressure here.*
"That sounds awful."	*No fix. No reframe. No silver lining. Just: what you experienced was real.*
"I can see you're done."	*Recognition without action. Their system hears: this person sees me.*

What empathy sounds like when it does not land:

What to avoid	What their system may hear
"I understand, but we still have to get dressed."	*The "but" can erase the empathy. Over time, it teaches them your empathy is a prelude to pressure.*
"I know this is hard. Let's just get through it together."	*Still carries an expectation. Their system may hear the demand, not the empathy.*
"I understand how you feel."	*Can feel too vague. Specificity communicates genuine attunement. Generality can feel like performance.*
"It's okay, there's nothing to worry about."	*Their nervous system is telling them otherwise. This can feel like being told their experience is wrong.*
"I know you don't want to, but you need to."	*Even gently, this pairs empathy with a demand. The demand is what lands.*

Your child is crying about socks. The socks are wrong. They were fine yesterday but they are wrong today. You have been through this before. You can feel the frustration building. You want to say "these socks are fine, just put them on, we're going to be late."

Instead, you sit down. You take a breath and actually try to feel what it is like to have something against your skin that your nervous system is screaming about, while someone stands over you telling you it is fine. You feel the shift in your own body. The frustration is still there but it has moved to the side. Something else has arrived: understanding. You look at your child and you say: "Something about this morning is really overwhelming." Then you wait.

That is Empathy.

L: Lower Demands

Core concept: systematically reducing the demand load based on your child's actual capacity. Not based on what "should" be manageable. Not based on what other children can handle. Not based on what they could do yesterday.

This is accurate load management, not permissiveness. You would not call a physical therapist permissive for not loading a recovering knee with the pre-injury weight. They assess current capacity and load accordingly. That is what competent load management looks like. You are doing the same thing with demand load.

Start with the demand audit. Look at your child's day from the moment they wake up to the moment they fall asleep. Count every demand. Explicit demands: the things you say out loud. Get dressed. Eat breakfast. Brush teeth. Get in the car. Sit down. Do homework. Say please. Make eye contact. Implicit demands: the things you expect without saying. That they will greet you in the morning. That they will sit at the table. That they will be in a reasonable mood. Invisible demands: the things you have not identified as demands. Your body language communicating urgency. The ambient pressure of a tidy house. The social performance expected when grandparents visit. The demand to transition from one activity to another. The demand embedded in "how was school?"

Count them all. The full worksheet is in the Appendix (Tool 3: 24-Hour Demand Snapshot). Most parents who complete it for the first time land somewhere between forty and eighty demands in a day. That number is always higher than expected. Not because parents are placing too many demands. Because nobody told them that the demands they considered normal were demands at all.

Now ask the key question about each one: what would actually happen if I dropped this demand today? Not what feels like it would happen. What would actually happen.

The bed is unmade. What actually happens? Nothing. The teeth are unbrushed this morning. What actually happens? They brush tonight. Breakfast was a granola bar in the car. What actually happens? They ate. They are not wearing matching socks. What actually happens? Absolutely nothing. They did not say please. What actually happens? They still received the thing and nobody's life changed.

For most demands on the list, the honest answer is: nothing catastrophic. The world adjusts. Standards shift. The things you thought were essential turn out to be cultural expectations or personal habits, not actual necessities. The genuinely non-negotiable demands in any given day are usually fewer than five: safety, essential medication, true physical necessities. Everything else is a candidate for reduction.

Declarative language is one of the most powerful tools in this pillar. It changes the demand load of a sentence without changing the information.

Instead of this	**Try this**
"Go brush your teeth."	*"The toothbrush is on the counter."*
"Come eat."	*"Breakfast is on the table."*
"Get ready to go."	*"The car leaves in ten minutes."*

"Feed the dog."	*"I notice the dog hasn't been fed yet."*
"Put your jacket on."	*"Your jacket is on the hook."*
"Go take a bath."	*"The bath is running."*
"Put your shoes on."	*"Your shoes are by the door."*
"Do your homework."	*"The homework folder is on the table."*
"Go to bed."	*"It's getting close to bedtime."*
"Do the dishes."	*"The dishes are still in the sink."*

Each pair contains the same information. The demand load is radically different. A direct command requires compliance. It narrows choice. It activates the autonomy-threat mechanism. Declarative language places information in the environment and leaves the response to the child. It communicates what exists without dictating what must happen. The child's nervous system encounters information, not instruction. That difference is the difference between a demand and an observation, and for a demand sensitive nervous system, it is enormous.

Your morning routine has fifteen steps. Today your child's window is narrow. You can see it in their face, their posture, the way they are moving. What actually has to happen before you leave the house? Clothes on their body. Shoes accessible. That is two demands instead of fifteen. The bed is unmade. The teeth are unbrushed. Breakfast was a granola bar. Nobody died.

That is Lower Demands.

A: Adjust

Core concept: every strategy is personalized to your child, based on what you know about their nervous system today. Not yesterday. Not last week. Today.

What works for one demand sensitive child may not work for yours. What worked for your child last Monday may not work this Monday. The Adjust pillar asks you to read where your child is right now, what their window looks like right now, what their interests are right now, and respond to that.

Interest bridges, not bribes. There is a critical difference and your child's nervous system knows which one it is encountering.

An interest bridge weaves your child's current interest into the demanded task. The interest is present during the demand, making the demand more tolerable. "Let's count Pokémon while we put shoes on." "Your character needs boots for the next level, right? Your boots are by the door." "I'm making pancakes that look like Minecraft creepers." The interest and the demand coexist. The interest does not depend on the demand being completed. It is alongside, not after.

A bribe attaches the interest as a reward for compliance. "If you put your shoes on, you can play Pokémon." "Finish your homework and you can have screen time." "Get dressed and we can make pancakes." The interest comes after the demand. It depends on compliance. The child's nervous system reads this accurately: the thing I want is being used as leverage. The demand is still a demand. The interest is a carrot, and carrots are contingencies, and contingencies are demands.

The difference matters because a bridge reduces the demand load of the task. A bribe adds a new demand (the demand to earn the reward) on top of the original one. Bridges work with PDA. Bribes work against it.

Adjust by the day. Their window varies. Their interests shift. Their capacity fluctuates based on sleep, on what happened at school, on the sensory load of the environment, on how many demands hit before the one you are presenting. The strategy that got them dressed on Monday may produce a blank stare on Wednesday. Not because Monday's strategy was wrong. Because Wednesday's nervous system is in a different state. Monday's performance is not evidence of Wednesday's capacity.

The capacity assumption is one of the most common and most damaging patterns in PDA parenting. "But they did it yesterday." That sentence, spoken or unspoken, communicates that yesterday's capacity is today's obligation. The child's nervous system reads it as a demand based on a false assumption, and the false assumption adds insult to injury. They know they could do it yesterday. They do not know why they cannot do it today. Your reminder that they could do it yesterday does not help. It increases the shame load on top of the demand load. Every day is a fresh read. What is the window today? What is the capacity today? Start there.

A warning about interest colonization. When you use a special interest as a bridge to demanded activities, the interest itself can become associated with demands in the child's nervous system. The safe space (Pokémon, Minecraft, dinosaurs, whatever the interest is) starts carrying demand residue. Your child may begin avoiding the interest itself, which is a significant loss because intense interests are one of the primary regulation tools for autistic and PDA children. If an interest bridge that was working stops working, the interest may have been colonized. Stop using that interest for demands entirely. Let it return to being a safe, self-directed space. Use a different interest for bridging, and do so more sparingly. The goal is connection through the interest, not compliance through it.

Adjust communication. Use the channel and framing that your child finds least demanding right now. Some children respond to indirect language: "I wonder if anyone wants toast" instead of "do you want toast?" Some respond to written notes left on the counter: a sticky note that says "shoes?" carries less demand than a verbal request because it does not require an immediate response to a person standing there waiting. Some need minimal words: "shoes" and a gesture toward the door. Some need communication through a shared interest: a reference to their game or their world that embeds the demand in familiar territory. Some need you to text them from the next room because the proximity of a person delivering a demand face-to-face is itself part of the threat.

The channel matters as much as the content. A demand delivered in the wrong channel can fail even when the demand itself is reasonable and the window is open. Experiment. Notice what works this week. Be ready for it to change next week.

Your child is fixated on a particular video game this week. Instead of pulling them away from it to get ready, you use it: "Your character needs boots for the next level, right? Your boots are by the door." The interest is the bridge. The demand is still there. Shoes need to go on. But the approach is adjusted to this child, this interest, this morning.

That is Adjust.

T: Time

Core concept: their nervous system needs more time than you think. More time than seems reasonable. More time than you are comfortable with. Build that time in anyway.

Remove visible time pressure. Stop referencing the clock. Stop the countdown. Every "five more minutes" is a demand. Every "we need to leave soon" is a demand. Every "we're going to be late" is a demand. Every glance at your watch that they can see is a demand. The urgency is real to you. The appointment exists. The school has a start time. But to their nervous system, each mention of time is another withdrawal from an already overdrawn account.

What to say: "There's no rush." "We have time." "Whenever you're ready." "No hurry." Even when those statements stretch the truth. The cost of time pressure on a demand sensitive nervous system is higher than the cost of being ten minutes late. Being late with a regulated child is better than being on time with a depleted one. Being late with an intact relationship is better than being on time after a battle that damaged it.

What not to say: "Five more minutes." "We're going to be late." "Hurry up." "Come on, let's go." "The bus is coming." "We need to leave by eight." "You have three minutes." "I'm counting to ten." Each of these is a demand that activates the threat response, which produces the opposite of what you want. You want them to move faster. Time pressure makes the nervous system freeze or fight. Freezing looks like they did not hear you. Fighting looks like a meltdown. Neither produces speed. Both cost more time than giving the time would have.

Recovery time after a hard moment is non-negotiable. After a meltdown, a difficult transition, a rupture, or any interaction that pushed the nervous system past its window, your child needs time that is genuinely free of demands. Not "take a minute and then we'll try again." That is a demand with a timer on it. That is not recovery. That is a brief pause before the next demand. Genuine recovery means: no one is waiting for them to be ready. No next step is hovering. No timer is running. Returning to the interaction is entirely their decision. Their timeline, not yours.

You can communicate the availability of recovery without making it a demand. "I'll be in the kitchen. Come find me if you want." That is genuine recovery offered. "Take five minutes and then we need to talk about this." That is a demand scheduled for five minutes from now. The difference is whether the return to engagement is their choice or your expectation.

Reframe the morning routine. If you are always rushing, the problem is not your child's speed. The routine has too many demands for the available window and the available time. The solution is not adding speed. It is never adding speed. The solution is removing demands or adding time, or both. Wake up earlier so the same number of steps has more space around them. Or reduce the number of steps so the same amount of time holds fewer demands. Or both.

You need to leave by 8:15. You used to start the morning routine at 7:45 and spend thirty minutes in escalating urgency. Now you start at 7:00 with two demands instead of fifteen and no clock references. Some mornings you are still late. But the mornings are no longer a battle. Your child arrives at school with a wider window instead of a depleted one. Your relationship did not take damage before 8 AM. The day starts differently, and differently compounds.

That is Time.

E: Environment

Core concept: the physical and social environment is placing demands on your child's nervous system that you may not have identified as demands. Every sensory input, every social expectation, every feature of the physical space is either adding to the demand load or reducing it.

Physical environment. Start with the senses. Overhead fluorescent lighting versus lamps: fluorescent light carries a flicker that many neurodivergent nervous systems register as a persistent low-grade stressor, even when the person is not consciously aware of it. Background noise versus quiet: a television running in another room, the hum of an appliance, a sibling playing music. Temperature. Textures against skin (clothing, furniture, bedding). Smells (cleaning products, cooking, perfume). Visual clutter: a counter covered in papers, a room full of objects, a wall full of posters and schedules and charts.

Each of these is a sensory demand. Your child may not be able to tell you which ones are contributing to their overwhelm. They may not know themselves. But their nervous system is tracking all of it. Small changes can reduce the ambient demand load before you have said a single word. Swap the overhead light for a lamp. Turn off the background television. Remove the visual clutter from the room where the hard things happen. Change the soap to something unscented. Put a soft rug where their feet land when they get out of bed. None of these feel like interventions. They are. Every sensory demand you remove is a withdrawal that did not happen, and that creates room in the budget for a demand that actually matters.

Social environment. How many people are in the room? Who is watching? Is someone expecting your child to perform? To be polite, to be engaged, to make eye contact, to participate, to demonstrate that they are having a good time? Social density is a demand. Audience is a demand. The presence of extended family, guests, unfamiliar people, or even familiar people who carry high expectations raises the social demand load significantly. Your child at home with you is one demand environment. Your child at Thanksgiving with twelve relatives is a completely different one. Plan accordingly. Pre-reduce demands on days with high social load. Give explicit exit permission before the event. Do not require them to greet, to hug, to sit at the table, to stay for dessert.

The retreat space. Every demand sensitive child needs a physical space that is genuinely demand-free. Not a "calm down corner" with a timer, a feelings chart, and an expectation that they will use it to regulate and then return to the activity. That is a demand-laden space dressed as a safe one. The timer is a demand. The feelings chart is a demand. The expectation of return is a demand.

A genuine retreat space is a place where absolutely nothing is required. No one asks when they are coming out. No one checks on them with questions. No one follows them in. No one monitors how long they have been there. The door closes and nothing follows them through it. The knowledge that this space exists, even when they are not using it, reduces the threat calculation running in the background of their nervous system. Escape routes reduce entrapment. The availability of exit reduces the need for exit.

The digital environment. Screens are simultaneously the highest-regulation and highest-demand environment many demand sensitive children inhabit. The game or video is self-directed, predictable, and controllable. For a nervous system that craves autonomy and predictability, screens provide exactly that. They are a regulation tool. The social and notification layers around the screen are something else entirely. Every notification is a demand. Every message is a potential social performance. The expectation of timely response is a temporal and social demand. Online social interactions carry all the same demands as in-person ones, plus the additional layer of asynchronous uncertainty: when will they reply? What did that message mean?

Understanding this distinction changes how you think about screen time. The screen itself may be regulating while the notifications and social expectations embedded in it are depleting. Screen time battles are rarely about screens. They are about losing a regulated space and entering an unregulated one. The demand audit applies here the same way it applies everywhere else. Help your child (when their window allows it) identify which parts of the digital environment are regulating and which are depleting. For younger children, you may need to observe and adjust: turning off notifications, limiting social apps while preserving the games and videos that regulate.

Predictability as regulation. The word "structure" makes most PDA parents flinch because every traditional professional told them "children need structure and consistency" and the structure made things worse. That is because those professionals meant compliance structure: rigid schedules, visual charts enforced as expectations, predictable consequences for unpredictable behavior. That kind of structure is a demand framework with pictures on it.

Nervous system structure is different. It means the environment is predictable. The relationship is predictable. You are predictable. Your child knows what to expect from the space, from the routine, and from you. That predictability lets the nervous system stop scanning for threat. It can relax the vigilance because the environment is known.

Routines are different from schedules. A schedule says "at 7:30 we do this." A routine says "after this, the next thing is usually that." Routines are sequenced but not time-bound. They remove the clock (which is a demand) while keeping the predictability (which is a regulation tool). Visual supports (picture schedules, written sequences, timers) can help as information tools the child can choose to reference. They become demands when you point to them and say "what's next?"

or use them to enforce compliance.

The most important form of predictability in your child's environment is you. When your child can predict how you will respond, because you respond from regulation rather than reacting from whatever state you happen to be in, you become the known quantity in an uncertain world. Your consistency is not about rules. It is about your state. A parent who responds predictably from a regulated nervous system is the most powerful environmental modification available. More powerful than the lighting. More powerful than the retreat space. Your predictability is a regulatory resource your child's nervous system can rely on. That consistency is what the nervous system needs. Not consistent rules. A consistent person.

Your child comes home from school and heads straight to their room. Instead of calling them to the kitchen for a snack and a conversation about their day, you leave a plate outside their door. The hallway light is off because overhead lights bother them after a full day of masking. You do not knock. Thirty minutes later, they emerge on their own.

That is Environment.

When the demand is truly non-negotiable

Some demands cannot be dropped. Safety situations. Essential medication. Medical procedures that have to happen. Legal requirements. When a demand is truly non-negotiable, everything else around it becomes the intervention.

Reduce all other demands that day. The medical appointment is non-negotiable. The bed, the teeth, the morning routine, the homework: all negotiable today. Clear the deck so the demand budget has room for the one thing that has to happen.

Give maximum time. Do not schedule the non-negotiable demand during a narrow window. Do not rush to it. Give as much lead time as the situation allows.

Give maximum control over process. "This has to happen today. You get to decide when, where, and how." The "what" is non-negotiable. Everything else is theirs.

Use every other pillar at full strength around the demand that cannot move. Empathy: "I know this is hard and I wish it didn't have to happen today." Lower Demands: nothing else is required of them today. Time: no clock pressure. Environment: the setting is as sensory-safe as you can make it. Relationship: you are there, present, regulated, and not adding anything beyond what is absolutely necessary.

Acknowledge that these moments will still be hard. They may still produce meltdowns. The goal is not compliance without distress. The goal is completing the necessary demand with the least possible damage to the nervous system and the relationship, and repairing afterward.

A note on Collaborative Problem Solving

If you are familiar with Ross Greene's Collaborative Problem Solving (CPS), the alignment with RELATE is genuine. CPS does not use behavioral leverage. It does not punish avoidance. It centers the child's experience.

But CPS requires conditions. It requires that both of you are within your windows of tolerance. It requires enough relational trust that problem-solving together does not feel like an interrogation. It requires that your child has sufficient window width to hold a collaborative conversation.

If you have tried CPS and it failed, it was probably not because your child "can't do CPS." It was because the conditions were not yet in place. RELATE creates those conditions. The relational deposits, the demand reduction, the widened window. When those conditions exist, CPS becomes a natural complement to RELATE. Treat the CPS conversation itself as a RELATE interaction: only when both of you are in your windows, released immediately if resistance appears, and never as a required activity. "I have some thoughts about how mornings work and I'd like to hear yours. Not right now if this isn't a good time." That is CPS inside RELATE.

Where to start

You do not need all six pillars working perfectly. Nobody does all six perfectly. The pillars are directions you move toward, not standards you achieve.

Start with two. Relationship first. Lower Demands second. Everything else builds on what those two establish.

Pick one pillar that feels most accessible right now. Try it once today. Not perfectly. Just once. See what shifts.

PART THREE

Chapter 9: ADAPT: When Things Go Sideways

The pillars are for the days when you have some room. When you can plan. When you can think about which pillar to lean on and which demand to lower and how to adjust the approach based on what you know about your child today.

ADAPT is for the moments when you have no room at all.

Your child is on the floor screaming. Or they have gone completely silent and will not respond to you. Or they are throwing things. Or they have locked themselves in their room and you can hear something breaking. Or they looked fine thirty seconds ago and now they are not fine and you do not know what happened.

ADAPT is a five-step protocol for in-the-moment crisis response. It is not a way to get compliance faster. It is a way to help your child's nervous system come back online without adding threat. Sometimes the result is that the original demand happens. Sometimes the result is that it does not happen today. Both are acceptable outcomes. The goal is the nervous system, not the task.

Step	What to do

A: Assess	*Read their body: escalating or shutting down? Then read yours. Regulate yourself first.*
D: Decrease	*Stop talking. Step back. Drop the demand. Drop all demands. Remove time pressure.*
A: Align	*Return their sense of control. Genuine choices only. Only when the system can receive them.*
P: Pace	*Wait. Be present and quiet. Do not fill the silence. The silence is the intervention.*
T: Test	*Smallest possible next thing. Not the original demand. If silence, wait more.*

Each step is expanded below. During a crisis, this table is all you need. Read it, run it, cycle through it. The detail is for after.

A: Assess

Read their body first. Are they escalating or shutting down? These are two different nervous system states and they need different things.

Escalation is the system mobilizing for fight or flight. You will see it in their body: tense muscles, clenched fists, raised voice, fast movements, pacing, aggression. The energy is up. The system is activated and looking for an exit or a target.

Shutdown is the system collapsing into conservation mode. You will see the opposite: flat affect, silence, stillness, withdrawn posture, eyes unfocused or averted, slow or absent responses. The energy is down. The system has decided that fighting and fleeing are not available and has gone into freeze or collapse.

You need to know which one you are looking at because your response is different. An escalated child needs space, reduced stimulation, and an exit. A shutdown child needs quiet presence, reduced demands, and time. Approaching an escalated child too closely adds threat. Leaving a shutdown child entirely alone can deepen the collapse.

Now read your own body. This is the step most parents skip and it is the most important one.

If your heart rate is up, if your jaw is tight, if your hands are clenched, if you can feel the urgency to fix this right now, you are activated. A dysregulated parent responding to a dysregulated child produces two dysregulated nervous systems driving each other further from the window. You already know what happens from here. The interaction escalates. The thing that was going to take ten minutes takes an hour. You end up in a repair cycle that costs more than the thirty seconds of breathing would have.

Regulate yourself first. Even thirty seconds. Breathe. Unclench your jaw. Drop your shoulders. Slow your movements. Sit down if you are standing, because standing over a dysregulated child is a threat signal regardless of what your voice is doing.

You are not doing this for yourself. You are doing this because your nervous system is about to be the first thing your child's nervous system encounters, and what it encounters determines what happens next.

D: Decrease

Your instinct in a crisis will be to add. Add instructions. Add explanations. Add consequences. Add reassurance. Add a plan. Resist that instinct. The nervous system is already overloaded. Adding anything, even helpful things, increases the load.

Instead, remove.

Stop talking. Most parents are talking too much during a crisis. Every sentence is a demand on a system that cannot process language at full capacity. The fewer words in the room, the less the nervous system has to manage.

Step back physically. If you are standing over them, you are a threat signal. Move away. Sit down. Get lower than them if you can. Reduce your physical presence in their space.

Drop the demand. Not modify it. Not postpone it. Drop it. "We don't need to figure this out right now." Say it and mean it. If you say it while internally still holding the demand, they will read the truth.

Drop all demands, not just the one that triggered the moment. This is the part that feels radical. The meltdown started because of shoes. But in the middle of the meltdown, asking about breakfast is also a demand. Mentioning the bus is a demand. Asking if they are okay is a demand. Reduce the total demand in the environment to as close to zero as you can get.

Remove time pressure. Stop referencing what needs to happen next. The clock is irrelevant to a nervous system in survival mode. Whatever was supposed to happen in ten minutes is not going to happen in ten minutes. Accepting that now saves you the escalation that comes from trying to hold the timeline.

"We don't need to figure this out right now." "There's no rush." "Nothing needs to happen." Those are decrease statements. They are removing things from the room, not adding them.

A: Align

Somewhere in this moment, your child lost their sense of control. That loss is what activated the threat response. Your job in this step is to give control back.

Offer genuine choices. Including the choice to do nothing.

"You're in charge of what happens next." But only say that if it is true. If the only acceptable outcome is compliance, the choice is fake and their nervous system will detect it instantly.

"Do you want to stay here or go somewhere quieter?" Genuine if both options are real.

"Is there anything that would make this feel okay, or is it just not happening today?" Genuine if "not happening today" is actually available to you.

"You don't have to decide right now." Genuine if you are willing to wait without hovering.

The key word is genuine. Every time. If "not today" is not an option you can live with, do not offer it. A fake choice detected by the threat-detection system confirms that the people around this child use the language of autonomy while withholding actual autonomy. That confirmation is worse than not offering the choice at all.

Genuine alignment might also sound like: "What would make this work for you?" or "Is there a version of this you could handle?" These are invitations to collaborate on the terms. They return agency to the person whose agency was threatened. Sometimes the answer is useful. Sometimes the answer is silence. Both responses are data.

P: Pace

Wait.

Regulation takes longer than you want it to. Longer than you think it should. Longer than feels reasonable. The silence will feel unbearable. You will want to fill it with words, with reassurance, with a plan, with "are you okay?" Resist all of it.

"Are you okay?" is a demand for a status report from a system that is not capable of generating one. "Do you want to talk about it?" is a demand to process an experience the system is still inside of. "What happened?" is a demand to narrate and explain something that occurred below conscious awareness.

Say nothing. Or say one thing: "I'm here. There's no rush." And then be quiet.

Their system is processing at its own pace. That pace is not negotiable. Rushing it restarts the cycle. Every intervention you add during the pace step, no matter how well-intentioned, is a demand that the system has to manage on top of whatever it is already managing. Less is more. Nothing is often best.

Be present. Be calm. Be quiet. Be available without being in their face. If they want you closer, they will signal it. If they need you further away, they will signal that too. Read the signal. Respond to it. Do not project your need for resolution onto their timeline for regulation.

This step is the hardest for most parents. The silence feels like inaction. It feels like you are not doing anything. You are doing the most important thing available: you are providing a calm, quiet, non-demanding presence while their nervous system finds its way back to the window. That is not nothing. That is the intervention.

T: Test

When you see signs of returning regulation (a shift in posture, a longer exhale, eye contact returning, a word or two, humor appearing, their body softening) try the smallest possible next thing.

Not the original demand. Something tiny and genuinely optional.

"I'm going to make toast. Want some?"

"I'm in the kitchen if you want to come hang out."

"There's water on the counter."

If the answer is no, or silence, you have not failed. You have learned "not yet." Wait more. Try again later with something even smaller. A test that reveals "not yet" is a successful test. It told you exactly what you needed to know: the window is not open enough for this yet.

The only failed test is one that demands too much too soon and restarts the cycle. If you test with the original demand ("Okay, are you ready to put your shoes on now?") you will likely restart the entire sequence from the beginning. The test is the smallest possible thing, not the thing you originally wanted.

Signs it is too soon to test: their body has not softened, their breathing has not deepened, they flinch or tense when you speak, they do not respond at all. Go back to Pace. Wait more.

ADAPT is cyclical

In real life, ADAPT rarely unfolds as a clean sequence from A to T. You will cycle through the steps multiple times. Assess, Decrease, wait. Assess again. Align, Assess. Test, realize it was too soon, Decrease again. This is not failure. This is accurate responsiveness. You are tracking your child's nervous system state in real time and adjusting. That is the skill. Not executing a perfect protocol. Reading the system and responding to what it is telling you.

Some cycles are short. Assess, Decrease, Pace, Test. Ten minutes. Window reopens. The demand happens.

Some cycles are long. Multiple passes through the steps over an hour. The demand does not happen today.

Both of those are ADAPT working.

A real example

Jordan is thirteen and has had a hard day. School, a doctor's appointment, and an unexpected schedule change. The family has a dinner out that Jordan previously agreed to. At 5:00 PM, Jordan announces they are not going.

Assess: Jordan is sitting rigidly on the couch, answering in short words. Mobilized but not in full meltdown. Cara, Jordan's stepparent, notices her own state. Anxious about being late. Jaw tight. Urgency rising. Cara takes a breath.

Decrease: Cara does not mention the time. She sits down in a chair across the room. Not beside Jordan. Not standing over them. She says: "Sounds like today got to be a lot." Then she says nothing.

Align: Three minutes of silence. Then Cara says: "You don't have to come tonight. I'd love it if you felt like it, but it's a genuine option." Jordan is quiet. Cara waits.

Pace: Seven more minutes of silence. Cara stays in the chair, relaxed. Jordan's posture shifts slightly.

Test: "I'm thinking about what might make tonight feel okay. Is there any version of dinner that could work, or is it just not the night?" Not "are you coming?" That demands a yes or no commitment. "Is there a version" opens possibility without requiring a specific answer.

Jordan: "I'd have to leave when I say."

Second cycle. Cara assesses. Jordan is beginning to come back to window. She decreases. Nothing added. "Absolutely. Your call on timing." She aligns. "What else would make it work? Your own transportation? Sitting where you want?"

Jordan names two more conditions. Cara paces. "Okay. We have twenty minutes before we'd need to leave for that to work. No pressure either way."

Cara leaves the room.

Jordan came. They left thirty minutes earlier than planned, which was one of Jordan's conditions. Cara noted afterward: "ADAPT worked. My own state was the hardest variable."

A real morning

Your child needs to get dressed. They are on the couch in pajamas, watching something on their tablet. They slept okay. Their window is somewhere in the middle. Not shutdown. Not flexible. You have checked your own state. You are tired but regulated. Here you go.

Cycle 1. You start with Empathy: "Mornings can feel really big." No response. You move to Adjust: their current interest is a particular game, so you have pre-selected a shirt with a character from it. You place it on the couch near them. Say nothing. You move to Time: no reference to the clock. You go back to the kitchen and make coffee. Be Near.

Five minutes pass. They have not moved. You Assess: posture has not changed, but they glanced at the shirt. Not ready but not refusing.

Cycle 2. You return with a low-demand offering (Offer Without Requiring): a piece of toast placed on the arm of the couch, no comment. You sit in the chair across the room and do something on your phone. Not watching them. Not waiting. Two minutes later, they eat the toast. That is data: the window is opening slightly.

Cycle 3. You use declarative language (Lower Demands): "The shirt is there when you want it. We have time." Then you leave the room again. Three minutes later you hear movement. They are putting the shirt on. You say nothing. They come to the kitchen. You hand them their shoes without a word. They put them on.

Total time: twenty-five minutes. Three passes through the cycle. The morning took longer than a compliance-based approach would have demanded. But your child arrived at school regulated instead of depleted. Nobody yelled. The relationship is intact. The demand budget has room left for whatever school requires.

The next morning, the same approach produces a different result. They do not put the shirt on. They do not eat the toast. They do not come to the kitchen. Their window is closed and it is staying closed. You Assess: this is not happening today. You text the school. You sit in the next room. You wait.

That is also ADAPT working.

Three passes through the same moment is RELATE working, not RELATE failing. Each cycle is informed by the last. Repetition with adjustment is the mechanism. The morning that took three cycles and twenty-five minutes in month one takes one cycle and eight minutes in month four. Not because your child changed. Because the relational environment became demonstrably safe.

PART THREE

Chapter 10: Daily Life Scenarios

The pillars are the framework. ADAPT is the crisis protocol. This chapter is where they meet your actual life.

Eight scenarios follow. Each one describes a situation you have probably lived through more than once. Each one walks through what most parents do (which makes sense from a neurotypical framework and does not work for this one), what RELATE suggests instead, and why the RELATE approach addresses the nervous system rather than the behavior.

These are not the only situations you will face. Your family has its own version of each one, and situations this book cannot anticipate. But the approach underneath is always the same: identify the demand load, identify which mechanism is driving the response (threat detection, Intolerance of Uncertainty, autonomy threat, or all three), reduce what you can, adjust what remains, and give the nervous system more time and space than feels reasonable.

Jump to the scenario closest to your hardest moment this week.

1. Morning Routine Meltdown

2. Homework Refusal

3. Hygiene Avoidance

4. Meltdown at a Family Event

5. Screen Time Battles

6. Sibling Conflict Over "Fairness"

7. School Refusal

8. Bedtime Resistance

1. Morning Routine Meltdown

Your child cannot start the day. Every step is a demand. The clock is the enemy.

The setup: It is 7:30 AM. Your child needs to be dressed, fed, teeth brushed, bag packed, and out the door by 8:15. They are still in bed, or on the couch in pajamas, or crying about something that seems insignificant to you. The clock is ticking. Your anxiety is rising. You can feel yourself starting to speed up, and every time you speed up, they slow down. Or stop entirely.

What you usually do: You repeat the checklist. You add urgency. You reference the time. "We have ten minutes." "You need to hurry." "The bus is coming." When nothing moves, you escalate. Your voice gets louder or tighter. You start doing things for them (pulling clothes over their head, shoving shoes on their feet) which produces either compliance-under-duress or a full meltdown. You arrive at school with both of you depleted and the day already damaged. Tomorrow morning you will do it again.

What RELATE suggests:

Start with Lower Demands. How many steps does your morning routine contain? Count them honestly. Wake up. Get out of bed. Use the bathroom. Wash hands. Get dressed (underwear, pants, shirt, socks, shoes: that is five demands inside one demand). Brush teeth. Brush hair. Eat breakfast (come to the table, choose food, eat, clean up). Pack bag. Get coat. Get to the car. That is fifteen to twenty demands before you leave the house.

How many of those are genuinely essential for leaving? Clothes on body. Shoes accessible. That is two.

Can they eat a granola bar in the car? Yes. Can they brush teeth tonight when the window is wider? Yes. Can the bed be unmade? Obviously. Can the hair be unbrushed? It will survive. Can they wear yesterday's shirt? Nobody at school will notice and if they do it does not matter. You have just reduced fifteen demands to two.

Apply Time. If you are always rushing, the routine has too many demands for the time available. Do not add speed. Add time or remove demands. Start at 7:00 instead of 7:45. The same two demands now have forty-five minutes of space around them instead of fifteen.

Remove all clock references. Do not say "we have ten minutes." Do not say "the bus is coming." Do not glance at the clock where they can see you. Use declarative language instead of commands. "Your clothes are on the chair." "There's toast on the counter." "The car will be ready when you are."

Apply Environment. Is the morning happening in a sensory-hostile space? Is the bathroom too bright? Is the kitchen noisy? Is the lighting overhead fluorescent? Is the house cold and the clothes feel wrong against their skin? Small environmental changes reduce the ambient load before anyone says a word.

Why it works: You have reduced the demand load from twenty items to two. You have removed time pressure. You have changed commands to declarative language. The nervous system encounters less threat in the first thirty minutes of the day. The morning is not pleasant. Some mornings it still does not go well. But it is no longer a daily battle, and your child arrives wherever they are going with something left in the budget instead of an empty account and a damaged relationship.

2. Homework Refusal

The demand to perform academic work after a full day of demands has exceeded capacity.

The setup: Your child has homework. They refuse to start. You know it needs to be done. They know it needs to be done. The standoff has been going on for twenty minutes. They are at the table with the worksheet in front of them, staring at it, or they have left the table entirely. You can feel the evening slipping away.

What you usually do: You negotiate. You threaten screen time loss. You sit with them and try to push through it together. You try the empathy-demand combination: "I know you don't feel like it, but let's just get it done." You end up doing most of it for them, or doing none of it and spending the rest of the evening in a standoff that poisons bedtime.

What RELATE suggests:

First, ask yourself the key question: what is the actual consequence of skipping homework tonight? If the answer is a note from the teacher, that is manageable. If the answer is a zero in the gradebook, decide whether the zero or the meltdown costs more. If the answer is genuinely nothing, release it.

If it matters enough to pursue, apply Adjust. Use an interest bridge. Can the math be done with Pokémon cards? Can the writing assignment be dictated while they move around the room? Can the reading be done as audiobook instead of eyes-on-page? The learning does not require sitting at a table with a pencil. The demand is the performance format (sitting, writing, compliance) not the learning itself. Change the format.

Apply Lower Demands. Can you do half tonight and half tomorrow? Can you scribe while they talk? Can the assignment be shortened by focusing on the parts that matter? "Do three problems instead of ten" is a demand reduction that often unlocks the window enough for all ten to happen once the initial resistance is past. "You don't have to do all of it" is sometimes the sentence that makes all of it possible.

Apply Time. Do not do homework immediately after school. The window is depleted from masking all day. Give recovery time first. Homework at 7 PM from a wider window produces better results than homework at 4 PM from a depleted one, even though it feels later than you would like.

If none of this works and the window is closed: the homework does not happen tonight. Email the teacher. "My child's capacity was not available tonight. We will try again tomorrow." You are not failing. You are reading the window accurately and responding to reality.

Why it works: You have separated the learning from the demand structure of homework. The demand was never the math. The demand was sit here, at this time, in this format, and produce. Reducing the format demands (through interest bridges, scribing, shortened assignments, flexible timing) makes the learning accessible without the full threat load.

3. Hygiene Avoidance

The bathroom is a sensory minefield. Every hygiene step is a demand.

The setup: Your child will not shower. Or brush their teeth. Or wash their hair. It has been days. You are worried about health. You are worried about what the school will say. You are worried about what the other parents think. Your own discomfort with the situation is growing.

What you usually do: You insist. You bargain. You disguise the demand as a question: "Wouldn't you feel better after a shower?" You know the answer is no, they would not, because the shower itself is the problem, not the outcome. Eventually you force the issue or give up and feel terrible about both options.

What RELATE suggests:

Apply Environment first. The bathroom is often the most sensory-hostile room in the house. Overhead lighting that buzzes. Tile that echoes. Water temperature that fluctuates. The texture of towels. The feeling of water hitting skin. The smell of soap or shampoo. The cold air on a wet body. Each of these is a sensory demand. Most parents have never audited the bathroom the way they would audit any other demand environment.

Identify which sensory elements are contributing and modify what you can. Swap the overhead light for a battery-operated lamp or a nightlight. Put a towel on the floor so their feet are not on cold tile. Find a soap and shampoo that do not have a strong smell. Let them control the water temperature completely. Warm the towel in the dryer first. These are not luxuries. They are demand reductions in a high-demand environment.

Apply Adjust. Modify the routine itself. A washcloth wipe-down instead of a shower. Dry shampoo instead of hair washing. Teeth brushed with water only if the toothpaste is the problem. A different toothbrush (softer, electric, finger brush). Teeth brushed in the kitchen instead of the bathroom if the bathroom is the trigger. Bathing in swimwear if the feeling of being naked in water is activating.

Apply Time. Not every hygiene task needs to happen every day. Teeth today, shower tomorrow. Hair twice a week instead of daily. Spread the tasks across days instead of stacking them. A child who brushes teeth three times a week and showers twice a week is meeting the basic health requirements. The daily standard is a cultural expectation, not a medical necessity. Reduce the frequency to match the capacity.

Apply Lower Demands with language. Do not say "go take a shower." Say "the shower is ready if you want it." Do not say "you need to brush your teeth." Say "the toothbrush is on the counter." If they do not engage, leave it. Try again tomorrow. The demand did not disappear. It moved to a different day, when the window might be wider.

Why it works: You have reduced the sensory demand of the environment, adjusted the method to what your child can tolerate, and spread the tasks across days instead of stacking them into a nightly ordeal. The hygiene happens. Not all of it. Not every day. But it happens, and nobody had to be held down or screamed at to make it happen.

4. Meltdown at a Family Event

Social demands, sensory input, and unfamiliar expectations have compounded past the window.

The setup: You are at a family gathering. Your child was doing okay for the first thirty minutes and then they were not. They are now escalating (yelling, crying, refusing to engage) or shutting down (hiding under a table, going nonverbal, clinging to you and refusing to interact with anyone) in front of extended family who do not understand PDA and are watching you parent. You can feel the judgment. Your own shame is rising. You are managing two things at once: your child's nervous system and your family's reaction.

What you usually do: You try to manage the meltdown quietly. You whisper threats or bribes that you know will not work but feel like the only tools available while twelve people are watching. You remove your child to another room while apologizing to the family. You feel the shame burning. You spend the drive home either furious or heartbroken or both. You wonder whether you should stop going to family events at all.

What RELATE suggests:

Apply ADAPT. This is a crisis moment. Run the protocol.

Assess: your child has hit their demand ceiling. The social performance (be polite, greet people, answer questions about school, tolerate hugs from relatives, sit at the table, use manners, be grateful) combined with the sensory load (noise, people, smells, unfamiliar physical space) has exceeded the window. Assess yourself: you are managing your own shame about being watched. That shame is activating your nervous system, which is transmitting activation to your child's system, which is making their crisis worse. Your regulation is the first priority, even before theirs.

Decrease: move to a quieter space. Not as punishment. Not "let's go to the other room until you calm down." Just move. "Let's go somewhere quieter." Or say nothing and lead them to a room with fewer people and less noise. Reduce the sensory input. Reduce the audience.

Align: give genuine exit permission. "We can leave whenever you need to." And mean it. If leaving is not actually an option you are willing to exercise, do not say it. But if it is, say it. "We can go right now if that's what you need." That sentence returns control. Their autonomy, which was stripped by every social expectation of the event, comes back.

Pace: do not rush them back to the group. Do not check the clock. Do not say "are you ready to go back in?" Do not ask if they want dessert or if they want to say goodbye. Just be with them in the quiet space. Wait.

Test: when you see signs of regulation (posture softening, breathing slowing, a word or two), offer one low-demand option. "Want to sit in the car with a snack for a while?" Not "are you ready to go back in?" The car is low-demand. The gathering is high-demand. Offer the low-demand option.

Why it works: You prioritized your child's nervous system over the social expectations of the event. The relatives may not understand. That is a separate problem for a separate day. Some of those relatives will never understand, and that is also information. The relevant question after a family event meltdown is not "why can't they handle it?" It is "what was the demand load of that environment and did anyone count it before we walked in?"

For future events: pre-reduce demands on the day of the event. Arrive with a plan for exit. Identify the quiet space before you need it. Give your child genuine permission to leave at any time. Do not require greeting, hugging, or performance. Brief your family in advance if they will hear it: "Our child may need to leave the room. That is normal for them. Please don't comment on it." Some family members will follow that request. Some will not. Plan for both.

5. Screen Time Battles

Screens are regulation, not reward. Removing them removes the coping strategy.

The setup: Your child has been on screens for hours. You want them to stop. They refuse. The transition away from the screen turns into the worst moment of the day, every day. You have read that screen time should be limited. You believe that. But enforcing the limit is costing more than the screen time itself.

What you usually do: You set a timer. You give warnings: "Five more minutes." "Two more minutes." "Time's up." You threaten to take the device. Eventually you take the device. A meltdown follows. The next hour is spent in crisis recovery. The screen time battle took longer and cost more than the screen time would have.

What RELATE suggests:

Start by reframing what screens are for your child. For many demand sensitive children, screens are not a treat, a reward, or a time-waster. They are a regulation tool. Screens provide a controlled, predictable, self-directed environment with minimal external demands. The child controls the pace, the content, the level of engagement. Nobody is asking them to perform. Nobody is placing expectations. The autonomy mechanism is quiet. The uncertainty mechanism is quiet. The threat-detection mechanism is quiet. Screens are the lowest-demand environment many PDA children have access to.

The demand to stop screens is high-threat because it requires leaving a safe, controlled space and entering an unpredictable one. The transition is from low demand to high demand. The nervous system resists that transition the same way it resists any demand: with the same mechanisms, the same intensity, the same fight-or-flight activation.

Instead of enforcing hard limits, negotiate transitions. "What feels like a good stopping point?" gives them control over the timing. "What would need to be true for you to feel ready to shift?" gives them input into the conditions. These are genuine questions, not disguised demands. If you ask "what feels like a good stopping point?" and then override their answer, you have taught them that the question was not genuine, and they will not engage with it next time.

Use interest bridges. Connect what they are doing on screen to what comes next, so the transition is not from their world to your world but a bridge between the two. If they are playing a building game, "I'm making dinner and I could use an architect" is an interest bridge. If they are watching a show, waiting for the end of an episode rather than pausing in the middle respects the structure they are engaged with.

Reduce the demand load of what follows the screen. If after screens they face a series of demands (dinner, homework, bath, bed), the nervous system is not resisting the end of screens. It is resisting the wall of demands on the other side. Reduce what follows. Make the post-screen environment as low-demand as possible. A transition from screen to another low-demand activity (a snack, free time, a walk) is easier than a transition from screen to compliance.

Why it works: You have stopped treating screens as the problem and started treating the transition as the demand. The battle was never about screen time. It was about the threat of losing a regulated space and entering an unregulated one. Addressing the transition (through negotiated timing, interest bridges, and reducing the demand load of what follows) addresses the actual mechanism.

6. Sibling Conflict Over "Fairness"

Your non-PDA child sees unfairness. Your PDA child sees threat. Both are accurate.

The setup: Your other child is watching the accommodations. The reduced demands. The flexible routines. The extra screen time. The things their PDA sibling "gets away with." They are angry. "That's not fair. How come they don't have to?"

What you usually do: You try to explain PDA to the sibling, but the explanation does not erase their experience of watching different rules apply. Or you swing the other way and crack down on the PDA child to make things "even," which produces a meltdown in the PDA child and does not actually satisfy the sibling because they can feel the inconsistency. Neither approach resolves the underlying problem, which is that your other child feels invisible and your PDA child's nervous system cannot tolerate the demands being imposed in the name of fairness.

What RELATE suggests:

Fair does not mean same. It means everyone gets what they need. Your non-PDA child needs this explained, but explanation alone is not enough. They need to see it in action for themselves, not just for their sibling.

Age-appropriate language helps: "Your sibling's brain works differently with expectations. That is why things look different for them sometimes. That does not mean your feelings matter less." Say this clearly. Say it more than once. And then back it up with action.

Give your non-PDA child their own accommodations. What is hard for them? What do they need more of? Dedicated one-on-one time with you that is not filtered through their sibling's needs. Their own version of flexibility where it matters to them. Permission to feel frustrated, jealous, and angry about the situation without being told they should understand or be patient. Their feelings about the inequity are valid. Telling them those feelings are wrong teaches them that their experience does not matter when their sibling's experience is in the room.

Protect one-on-one time with each child. Even fifteen minutes where your non-PDA child has your undivided attention. It does not have to be elaborate. It does not have to be an outing. It has to be theirs. Uninterrupted. Not rescheduled because the PDA sibling had a crisis. That last part is the hardest, and it is the most important. If one-on-one time with your non-PDA child is consistently sacrificed for the PDA child's needs, the sibling's experience of invisibility is being confirmed, not addressed.

If the sibling dynamic is creating persistent distress (one child consistently withdrawing, acting out, or expressing a sense of unfairness that feels stuck rather than passing), family therapy with a provider who understands PDA and family systems can help. This is not a sign that you have failed to balance things. It is a sign that the situation is genuinely difficult and the whole family could use support navigating it.

Why it works: You have addressed your non-PDA child's real need, which is not identical treatment but their own recognition and relationship with you. You have given them permission to feel what they feel. And you have not removed accommodations that your PDA child's nervous system requires in order to create an appearance of fairness that would cost everyone more than it gains.

7. School Refusal

Cumulative demand load has exceeded capacity. This is not about the school itself.

The setup: Your child will not go to school. Not today. Not this week. Maybe not at all. You are getting calls from the school. You are worried about truancy. You are worried about falling behind. You are worried about the future. You are running out of ideas and running out of patience.

What you usually do: You force it. You drag them to the car. You bribe them with something for after school. You make deals: "Just go for the morning." You push through the resistance because the alternative feels like giving up. Or you give in and spend the day consumed by anxiety about what it means that your child is not in school, and whether this is the beginning of something permanent.

What RELATE suggests:

School refusal in PDA is rarely about the school itself. It is about cumulative demand load exceeding the window. School is a multi-hour, high-demand environment. Social performance. Schedule compliance. Sensory overload. Transitions every forty-five minutes. Instruction-following. Sitting still. Eye contact. Raising your hand. Waiting your turn. Producing work on demand. Performing comprehension. Navigating the cafeteria. Managing the hallway. Every single one of those is a demand. By the time your child gets home, the window may be fully depleted. If home also carries heavy demands, there is no recovery space and the system eventually crashes. School refusal is the crash.

Start by reducing home demands. Freeing capacity at home can sometimes free enough capacity for school. If the evenings are full of homework battles, hygiene demands, and bedtime struggles, the child's nervous system is getting no recovery between one school day and the next. Reduce the evening demand load. Let homework go. Let bedtime flex. Let the evening be as close to demand-free as you can make it. Sometimes that recovered capacity is enough to make the next school day survivable.

If it is not enough, consider whether partial attendance is the accurate answer right now. Two hours of school with a wider window is more productive than six hours of masking followed by a collapse. Many schools will work with you on modified schedules if you bring data and specific requests. "My child can attend from 10 to 12 with a reduced academic load" is a specific, manageable request. "My child needs a completely different approach" is not. Start with the specific request. Build from there.

Work with the school on what is possible. Chapter 16 gives you language for that conversation. Bring your demand audit data. Show the school how many demands the school day contains. The number is often shocking to professionals who have never counted. Lead with the mechanism: "My child's nervous system processes demands as threats. Here is what the demand load of a school day looks like. Here is what we are seeing at home as a result."

If your child cannot attend at all right now, that is information about the demand load, not information about your child's character or your parenting. Some demand sensitive children need a period of demand recovery before school attendance is possible again. That period may be weeks. It may be months. Forcing attendance during that period does not build tolerance. It deepens the depletion and extends the recovery timeline.

Why it works: You have stopped treating school attendance as a behavior problem and started treating it as a capacity problem. The question is not "how do I make them go?" It is "what would the total demand load need to look like for attending to be within their window?" That question has answers. The other question does not.

8. Bedtime Resistance

The demand load of a bedtime routine is invisible until you count the steps.

The setup: Bedtime is a nightly ordeal. The routine takes an hour, sometimes ninety minutes. There are negotiations about every step. You end the day exhausted and dreading doing it again tomorrow. By the time they are finally asleep, you are too depleted to do anything for yourself. You lie on the couch feeling like the day took everything and gave nothing back.

What you usually do: You enforce the routine. You add consequences for stalling. You give in on some steps and then feel resentful about it. You alternate between rigid and permissive depending on how much energy you have left, which means your child's nervous system encounters a different parent every night, which increases the uncertainty load, which makes bedtime harder, which depletes you further. The cycle feeds itself.

What RELATE suggests:

Start by demand-auditing the bedtime routine. How many steps does it actually contain? Pajamas. Teeth. Face wash. Toilet. Book. Lights. Prayer. Tuck-in. Water. One more hug. Another question. Another drink of water. Fixing the blanket. The stuffed animal that needs to be in the right position. The door that needs to be open exactly the right amount.

Each step is a demand. Some of them are demands you placed. Some of them are demands your child placed on themselves (the stuffed animal, the door) which are actually regulation rituals, and those should not be touched.

Which steps are genuinely essential? The goal of bedtime is eventual sleep, not the performance of a bedtime routine. Sleep requires: a safe place to lie down and enough nervous system regulation to let go of wakefulness. That is it. Everything else is either a demand you can reduce or a regulation ritual you should leave alone.

Apply Lower Demands. Can they sleep in tomorrow's clothes, skipping the pajama demand entirely? Can teeth happen earlier in the evening when the window was wider, decoupling it from the bedtime sequence? Can the book be an audiobook they control instead of a read-aloud that depends on your presence and your pacing? Can the routine be reduced to: go to your room, your audiobook is ready, goodnight? Two demands instead of fifteen.

Apply Environment. Is the bedroom sensory-safe for sleep? Is the lighting too bright? Are they expected to fall asleep in total darkness when their nervous system needs some light? Is the room too quiet (some children need white noise or background sound) or too loud? Is the temperature right? Is the bedding tolerable against their skin? Small environmental changes reduce the sensory demand of the sleep space, which makes the transition to sleep less threatening.

Apply Time. Start earlier so there is no time pressure. If bedtime takes an hour, begin the wind-down an hour before you want them asleep. Do not announce "it's bedtime" at 8:00 and then spend sixty minutes in a struggle. Begin reducing the demand load of the evening at 7:00 (lower lights, quieter activities, fewer demands, no new tasks) and let bedtime emerge from the wind-down rather than arriving as a sudden transition from activity to compliance.

Do not reference the clock. "It's 8:30, you need to be in bed" is a demand. "Your room is ready when you are" is an observation. "It's getting late" is time pressure. "I'm heading to bed soon, goodnight when you're ready" communicates the approaching end of the day without demanding compliance with it.

Why it works: You have reduced the bedtime demand load to its essentials, modified the sensory environment to support sleep rather than fight it, and removed the time pressure that was turning every evening into a siege. Sleep eventually happens. It may not happen at the time you want. It may not follow the routine you imagined. But it happens, and nobody is in tears, and the relationship did not take damage in the last hour of the day.

The approach underneath all eight

Every scenario in this chapter has the same answer underneath it. Identify the demand load. Identify which mechanism is driving the response. Reduce what you can. Adjust what remains. Give the nervous system more time and space than feels reasonable. Protect the relationship over the task.

Sometimes RELATE does not produce the outcome you wanted. The homework does not get done. The shower does not happen. The family event ends early. The school attendance does not resume this week. None of that means you failed. It is the honest reality of supporting a nervous system that processes demands as threats.

The question is not "did the task happen?" The question is "did I respond to the nervous system instead of the behavior?"

If you responded to the nervous system: you did the right thing. The task will come back around. The nervous system's trust in you compounds. The window widens over time. The things that were impossible this month become possible in three months, not because you forced them, but because you created the conditions in which capacity could build.

PART THREE

Chapter 11: The Playbook

This is the chapter you keep on your nightstand.

Everything before this was understanding: what demand sensitivity is, why your child responds the way they do, how the framework works, what to do in specific scenarios. You needed that understanding because without it, the plays in this chapter are just phrases someone told you to say. With the understanding, they are tools connected to a mechanism. You know why they work. That knowledge makes them land differently when you use them.

But right now, at 7:30 AM with your child on the floor, you do not need to review the mechanism. You need words. You need to know what to say, what not to say, what to do, and what not to do. That is what this chapter is.

It is organized by the moment you are in, not by concept. Find your situation. Use what fits. Come back when the moment has passed and read the chapters that explain why it worked.

A note before you start. These are not scripts to memorize. They are plays to reference. You will not remember all of them. You do not need to. Read them now. Read them again tomorrow. Say a few of them out loud to yourself when you are alone, because language that has been spoken out loud is more available under stress than language that has only been read silently. Pick three phrases from any section. Say them in the shower, in the car, wherever you will not feel self-conscious. Say them until they feel natural. Then, the next time your system is activated and you need words, they will be there. Not because you memorized them. Because your brain has a path to them that did not exist before. That is how language becomes available under stress. Not through reading. Through repetition.

When they are melting down

The nervous system is in fight-or-flight. The thinking brain is offline. They cannot process logic, reason, or explanation. They may not be able to process language at all. Your job is to reduce threat, not resolve the situation.

What to say:

"I'm here."

"There's no rush."

"You don't have to talk."

"We don't need to figure this out right now."

"I'm going to sit here. You're safe."

"Nothing needs to happen right now."

"I'm not going anywhere."

"Take all the time you need."

These sentences share a structure: they remove demands from the environment. They communicate presence without requiring anything in return. They are short because a nervous system in crisis cannot process long sentences. They do not ask questions. They do not require responses. They are offerings of safety, not requests for engagement.

What not to say:

"Calm down." (A demand to regulate a system that has lost the ability to regulate on command. The two most counterproductive words available.)

"Use your words." (A demand for language production from a brain that has taken language partially offline.)

"You're okay." (Invalidation. They are not okay. Their nervous system is telling them they are in danger. Telling them otherwise tells them you cannot read the room.)

"Take a deep breath." (A demand. Even a well-intentioned one. Their breathing will regulate when their system regulates. Instructing them to breathe adds a task to a system that cannot hold tasks.)

"If you don't stop, we're leaving." (A threat on top of a threat. Escalates the activation.)

"What happened?" (A demand to narrate and explain an experience that occurred below conscious awareness. They may not know what happened. The question requires retrieval, organization, and verbal production from a brain that is not capable of any of those right now.)

"I need you to stop." (A demand that communicates your needs are the priority. Their nervous system hears: even when I am in crisis, this person needs something from me.)

"We talked about this." (A reference to a previous conversation that requires memory retrieval and cognitive context-switching. Completely unavailable during activation. Also carries the implicit demand: you should know better.)

What to do:

Stop talking. Less is almost always more during a meltdown. Silence from a calm presence is more regulating than any words.

Sit down. Get physically lower than them if you can. Standing over a dysregulated person is a threat signal regardless of your tone or your intentions. Your height communicates authority and power. Sitting or crouching communicates availability without dominance.

Remove the audience. If other people are watching (siblings, relatives, classmates, strangers) move to a space with fewer eyes. The social demand of being watched during a crisis compounds the activation.

Remove time pressure. Whatever was supposed to happen next is not happening next. Accept that now. The appointment, the school, the dinner, the plan. Let it go. It will still be there when the crisis passes.

Do not touch unless they reach for you. Physical contact during a meltdown can escalate the activation if the child is in a state where proximity is threatening. If they reach for you, receive it. If they do not, keep your body available without initiating contact.

Wait. Longer than you want to. Longer than feels productive. The meltdown has a physiological arc. The stress hormones need time to clear the system. You cannot speed that process. You can avoid extending it by not adding demands. Waiting feels like doing nothing. It is the most important thing available.

What not to do:

Reason. ("If you just put your shoes on, we can go to the park and you'll have fun." Logic requires the prefrontal cortex. It is offline.)

Explain. ("The reason we need to go is because..." Explanation is a demand for processing.)

Lecture. ("This is the third time this week that..." Historical context requires memory retrieval and carries implicit shame.)

Reference what caused it. ("This is all because of the socks." Identifying the trigger does not help them regulate. It adds a demand to evaluate your assessment.)

Ask them to name what they are feeling. ("Can you tell me what you're feeling right now?" Emotional identification and labeling require cognitive resources that are not available.)

Try to fix it. Your instinct is to solve the problem. The problem right now is not the socks or the homework or the schedule. The problem is a nervous system in survival mode. The fix is time and reduced threat, not solutions to the triggering demand.

When they are shutting down

Shutdown is different from meltdown. The energy is down, not up. The nervous system has decided that fighting and fleeing are not available and has collapsed into conservation mode. Flat affect. Silence. Stillness. Glazed eyes. Withdrawal. They may appear calm from the outside. They are not calm. They are in freeze.

What to say:

Almost nothing. Shutdown means the system is conserving. Additional input, even gentle input, is additional load.

> "I'm in the next room if you need me." (Communicates availability without requiring proximity.)
>
> "There's food on the counter." (Meets a basic need without requiring them to come to you or respond.)
>
> "No rush." (Two words. Removes time pressure.)

Or say nothing at all. Leave a glass of water within reach. Leave a blanket nearby. Leave the room if your presence is adding to the load. Your absence can be more regulating than your presence during shutdown, because your presence carries the implicit demand of someone waiting for you to come back online.

What not to say:

"What's wrong?" (A demand to identify, articulate, and share their internal state. During shutdown, they may not have access to that information themselves.)

"Talk to me." (A direct demand for verbal production from a system that has taken verbal production offline.)

"You can't just sit there." (A demand to produce visible activity. They are not just sitting there. They are in freeze. It is a nervous system state, not a choice.)

"We need to deal with this." (A demand to engage with a problem while the system is in conservation mode. Everything about this sentence communicates that their current state is insufficient and they need to produce something different.)

"How can I help?" (Sounds compassionate. Is a demand. It requires them to assess their needs, identify what would help, formulate a response, and deliver it. During shutdown, none of those steps are available.)

What to do:

Reduce sensory input. Lower the lights. Turn off noise. Reduce the number of people in the space. The nervous system in freeze is overwhelmed. Every sensory input is a load.

Place food and water within reach without comment. Do not bring it to them with eye contact and a "here you go." Set it down nearby. Walk away. They will eat or drink when their system has recovered enough to manage it.

Be available without being present if your presence is adding demand. Some children in shutdown need a person nearby. Some need to be alone. Read which one yours needs right now. If you are unsure, default to nearby but not in the room. Door open. You in the next space. Reachable but not watching.

Wait longer than feels reasonable. Shutdown can last minutes or hours. The timeline is not yours. Do not set a timer on it. Do not check in every ten minutes to see if they are "better." Each check-in is a demand. Let the recovery happen at the pace the nervous system requires.

What not to do:

Pursue them. If they have gone to their room and closed the door, do not knock repeatedly. Do not open the door to check on them. Do not stand outside the door where they can hear you breathing. The closed door is communication: I need to not be accessible right now. Respect it.

Set a timer on recovery. "You can have fifteen minutes and then we need to talk." That is a demand hovering over the recovery space. Recovery that has a deadline is not recovery.

Require them to come out for meals. Bring food to them. Or leave it outside their door. The demand to come to the table, to sit with the family, to perform normalcy, is not appropriate during shutdown.

Interpret shutdown as manipulation. "They're just doing this to get out of it." Shutdown is not a strategy. It is a nervous system state. The child in freeze is not calculating. They have left the building, neurologically speaking. They will come back when the system allows it.

When they refuse something they need to do

The demand is real. The teeth need brushing. The medicine needs taking. The clothes need to go on. But the window is narrow and the direct approach is not working.

What to say:

Switch to declarative language. Place information in the environment and let their system decide when to act.

Declarative language for this moment	
"The toothbrush is on the counter."	*Information, not instruction.*
"Your shoes are by the door."	*Available, not required.*
"The medicine is on the table."	*Present, not demanded.*
"Your clothes are on the chair."	*Placed, not pushed.*
"The car is ready when you are."	*Timeline is theirs.*
"Breakfast is on the counter."	*Offered, not enforced.*

These sentences give the same information as a direct command without the demand structure of a command. "The toothbrush is on the counter" and "go brush your teeth" contain identical information. The demand load is completely different.

If declarative language does not produce movement, reduce further.

If you need to go further	What it opens
"Is there a version of this that would work?"	*Negotiation on terms without removing the demand.*
"What would make this easier?"	*Genuine question. Accept "nothing" as data.*
"Would it help if I did part of it?"	*Sharing the load. Scribing, laying out clothes, toothpaste on the brush.*
"This needs to happen today. You get to decide when and how."	*Honest about the requirement. Autonomy over process.*

What not to say:

What to avoid	What their system hears
"Go brush your teeth." "Put your shoes on." "Get dressed."	*Direct commands carry the highest demand load. The autonomy-threat mechanism activates immediately.*
"You need to do this."	*The word "need" signals that their choice has been removed.*
"Just do it and it'll be over."	*This can feel dismissive of how hard it actually is for them right now.*
"But you did it yesterday."	*Yesterday's window is not today's. This can add shame on top of the demand.*

"I'm not asking much."	*What feels small to you may feel overwhelming to their system right now.*

What to do:

Ask yourself the key question: what would actually happen if this did not happen right now? If the answer is nothing dangerous, release it. Try again later or tomorrow.

If it is non-negotiable (medication, safety) reduce everything else. Clear the deck. Give maximum time. Give maximum control over process.

Use an interest bridge if their interest is accessible. Embed the demand inside something familiar and regulated.

Modify the method. A washcloth instead of a shower. Clothes that are easier to put on. Medicine mixed into a drink. The goal is the outcome, not the performance of the standard method.

What not to do:

Repeat the demand. Each repetition doubles the demand load. By the third ask, your child is managing not just the original demand but the escalating pressure of your frustration.

Add consequences. "If you don't brush your teeth, no screen time." Now the child is managing the original demand plus the threat of loss. Two demands instead of one. Neither gets met.

Stand and wait. Your physical presence, standing there watching them not do the thing, is a demand. Walk away. Come back later. Give the demand room to breathe.

When they refuse something they want to do

This is the most confusing scenario for parents. They asked to go to the park. You said yes. Now they cannot get in the car.

What to say:

"The option is there if you want it. No pressure either way."

"We can try again another time."

"You don't have to decide right now."

"It's okay to want something and not be able to do it right now. Those are two different things."

That last sentence is one of the most important things you can say to a demand sensitive child. It names the experience they are having: wanting something and being unable to tolerate the demands of doing it. Most people treat those as contradictory. They are not. They are two systems producing contradictory outputs, and naming that honestly is more validating than any other response.

What not to say:

What to avoid	What it can feel like to them
"But you said you wanted to go!"	*This frames their state as inconsistency. They did want to go. They still do. The demand activated the threat response.*
"You're going to miss out."	*Adds fear-of-missing-out pressure on top of what they are already carrying.*
"We already paid for this."	*Financial guilt becomes another weight. The money is gone either way.*

"We planned this whole thing for you."	*Adds the burden of gratitude and the feeling of having let people down.*
"Fine, then we're never doing this again."	*This can teach them that wanting things is risky, because not being able to follow through gets punished.*

What to do:

Understand the mechanism. The desire did not change. The demand changed. The moment the activity shifted from "I want to" to "I have to" (even if the "have to" was just the implicit expectation created by saying yes), the threat response activated. This is Mechanism 3 (perceived loss of autonomy) in its purest form.

Let it go without commentary. Do not process it. Do not debrief it. Do not explain to them why it happened. They know it happened. They are living inside the contradiction. Adding your analysis of it is another demand.

Keep the option alive without attaching expectation. "The park isn't going anywhere. We can try whenever." That communicates that the opportunity is not closed and they are not being punished for this moment.

What not to do:

Try to push through. ("Come on, once we're there you'll have fun." Maybe. Maybe not. Pushing a nervous system past its current window on the gamble that it will regulate once the environment changes is a gamble that fails more often than it succeeds with PDA. When it fails, the meltdown happens at the park, far from home, with an audience.)

Make it a pattern narrative. ("You always do this. Every time we plan something." Even if it is true, saying it aloud attaches a story of inevitability to the experience. The child hears: this is who I am. I am the person who cannot do things.)

Withdraw. (Going silent. Becoming visibly disappointed. Leaving the room in frustration. Your disappointment is a demand. It communicates: you let me down. That communication goes straight to the nervous system as relational threat.)

When you have lost your temper

You yelled. You said something you did not mean. You escalated when you knew you should not have. You grabbed their arm or slammed a door or said the thing that landed on their face like a slap. It happened. You cannot undo it. What you do next matters more than what you just did.

What to say (later, on their timeline, not yours):

Repair language	What it communicates
"I pushed too hard earlier. I'm sorry. You don't need to say anything about it."	*Names it. Owns it. Removes the demand to respond.*
"That wasn't okay. I was frustrated and I put that on you. That's on me."	*Takes full responsibility. No shared blame.*
"I can see that what I did earlier made things harder. I want to do it differently next time."	*Validates their experience of the rupture.*
"I got caught up in the schedule and forgot that you needed more time. I'm sorry."	*Specific. Shows you understand what happened.*

"I think I made that feel like you had no choice. That wasn't what I meant, and I'm going to work on that."	*Commitment to change, not just words.*

These repairs share a structure: they name what happened specifically, they own it without justification, and they do not require a response. The child does not need to say "it's okay." The child does not need to forgive you. The child does not need to acknowledge the repair. The repair is something you offer. It is not a transaction.

What not to say:

What to avoid	Why it can land differently than intended
"I'm sorry, but you weren't listening."	*The "but" shifts some of the responsibility back to them. It can undo the apology.*
"I said I'm sorry, can we move on?"	*This can feel like a demand for closure on your timeline, not theirs.*
"Are we okay?"	*Asking for reassurance puts the work of resolving your guilt on them.*
"I'm sorry you felt that way."	*This does not actually own what happened. It can feel like a non-apology.*
"I already apologized."	*This can communicate that their ongoing feelings about it are unreasonable.*

What to do:

Wait. Do not repair immediately. If your child is still activated, the repair is another demand. It requires them to receive your words, process your apology, and generate some response. Wait for the window to open. The timing belongs to their system, not your discomfort.

Repair without requiring their participation. Say what you need to say. Then stop. If they do not respond, the repair still landed. Their nervous system heard it even if their mouth did not acknowledge it.

Change the behavior, not just the words. Verbal repair followed by behavioral repetition is not repair. If you apologize for yelling and then yell again tomorrow, the apology means nothing. Changed behavior over time is the repair that counts. The words are the beginning. The behavior is the proof.

What not to do:

Require them to apologize back. Forced apologies are demands, not repair. If your child apologizes on their own, it is meaningful. If you require it, it is a performance to satisfy your need for symmetry.

Process it as a couple in front of them. ("I shouldn't have done that, should I?" to your partner, while the child is in earshot. That is not repair. That is using the child's presence to perform accountability without actually engaging with the child.)

Use the repair as a teaching moment. ("When people make mistakes, we say sorry. I made a mistake, so I'm saying sorry." The child does not need a lesson on social norms. They need you to own what happened without attaching curriculum to it.)

When the morning is falling apart

It is happening right now. You need something in the next sixty seconds.

What to say:

"Morning." (And nothing else. Make coffee. Be present. Do not perform.)

"Your clothes are on the chair." (Declarative. Not a command.)

"There's toast on the counter." (Availability, not instruction.)

"We have time." (Even if it is a stretch. The cost of time pressure is higher than the cost of being late.)

"What would help right now?" (Genuine. If the answer is "leave me alone," leave them alone.)

What not to say:

"Good morning! Did you sleep okay? What do you want for breakfast? Don't forget you have that thing today." (Four demands before their feet hit the floor.)

"We're going to be late." "The bus is coming." "Hurry up." "Come on." (Time pressure. Activates freeze or fight. Produces the opposite of speed.)

"Why aren't you dressed yet?" (A demand for self-analysis. Also communicates frustration disguised as a question.)

What to do:

Cut the routine to two demands: clothes on body, shoes accessible. Everything else can be dropped, moved, or simplified. The morning will not be perfect. It does not have to be. It has to be survivable without damaging the relationship or depleting the demand budget before the day has started.

When you are in public

The meltdown is happening at the store, the restaurant, the parking lot. People are watching.

What to say:

"We can leave whenever you need to." And mean it.

"Want to go sit in the car for a bit?"

"I'm right here."

"Let's go somewhere quieter."

What not to say:

"People are watching." (Adds social shame as a demand.)

"Not here." (Communicates that their nervous system state is a performance problem, not a real experience.)

"You need to hold it together." (A demand to suppress a physiological response. Equivalent to telling someone to hold in a sneeze.)

"We'll deal with this when we get home." (A deferred threat. Their nervous system now has to carry the current crisis plus the anticipation of consequences.)

What to do:

Prioritize their nervous system over the social expectations of the setting. Move to a quieter space. Give genuine exit permission. Leave the cart. Leave the restaurant. Leave the party. The groceries will wait. The meal can be boxed up. The social obligation can be repaired later. Your child's nervous system cannot wait.

Manage your own shame first. The people watching are activating your nervous system. Your activation is transmitting to your child. The shame spiral (they are watching me fail as a parent) produces urgency in you, which produces escalation in them, which produces more watching. Break the loop by attending to your own state before attending to theirs. One breath. Drop your shoulders. Then move to your child.

What not to do:

Whisper threats. ("If you don't stop right now, we are going home and there will be no screen time for a week." Whispered threats are still threats. The whispering adds a layer of social shame: I do not want people to hear how I am handling this.)

Apologize to the audience. ("I'm sorry, they're having a hard day." Your child hears: my parent is apologizing for my existence. That is a relational injury on top of a nervous system crisis.)

Perform calm for the watchers. ("It's okay sweetie, let's use our calm-down strategies." Said in a voice calibrated for the audience, not the child. The performance is readable. The child knows it is not for them.)

What to say to yourself

Your internal narrative drives your state. Your state drives what your child's nervous system encounters. What you say to yourself in the hard moments is not self-help. It is part of the mechanism.

> "This is a hard moment, not a crisis."
>
> "Connection, not compliance."
>
> "I am the lever, not the problem."
>
> "Their behavior is a signal, not an attack."
>
> "What does their nervous system need right now? Not what do I need them to do."
>
> "I don't have to fix this. I have to survive it without making it worse."
>
> "Regulate first. Everything else comes after."

"The goal right now is the relationship, not the task."

"I can try again tomorrow."

"This is the mechanism. Their system is in threat mode. This is not personal."

"I can't regulate them. I can only regulate me."

"Nothing useful happens from this state. Breathe first."

"What would I do right now if I weren't afraid?"

"This moment will end. The relationship won't, unless I damage it."

"I have survived every hard moment so far. This one is not different."

"Progress is invisible until it isn't. That doesn't mean it isn't happening."

"I don't need them to be okay right now. I need me to be okay right now."

"What's the demand I'm placing on myself in this moment? Can I drop it?"

"They are not giving me a hard time. They are having a hard time."

"The fact that I'm thinking about this at all means I'm doing something right."

These are not affirmations. They are recalibrations. Short sentences that pull your nervous system back toward the window when everything in you is saying this is falling apart. Pick three. Say them out loud ten times. They will be available to you when you need them if you have practiced them when you did not.

What to say to the people around you

Not everyone in your child's life understands demand sensitivity. Most do not. You will need language for the people who matter: grandparents, teachers, partners, siblings, friends, coaches, therapists.

The one-sentence opener:

"My child's nervous system processes demands as threats."

That single sentence opens more doors than a diagnosis code. It is specific enough to be meaningful and accessible enough to be understood by someone who has never heard of PDA. Use it as the starting point for any conversation about your child's needs.

To grandparents and extended family:

"Their brain works differently with expectations. What looks like defiance is actually anxiety. We're following our clinician's guidance."

You do not need to convince them. You do not need them to understand PDA. You need them to follow specific behavioral guidelines: what to say, what not to say, what demands not to place. That is a more achievable ask than changing their belief system.

"Please don't ask them questions when they first arrive. Give them time to settle in."

"If they go to another room, that's okay. Please don't follow them or ask them to come back."

"Please don't comment on what they're eating or not eating."

Specific, behavioral, actionable. Not a lecture about neurodivergence. A set of instructions that protect your child's demand environment during the visit.

To teachers and school staff:

"Can we start with one small accommodation and build from there?"

Bring the One-Page Summary from the Appendix (Tool 8). It gives the school everything they need on one sheet: what helps, what makes things harder, what escalation and shutdown look like, what to do and what not to do.

"My child can handle the academic content. The demand structure of the school day is what exceeds their capacity."

"When they refuse, it is not defiance. Their nervous system has activated a threat response. The thinking brain is not available."

"Consequences for demand avoidance will increase the avoidance, not decrease it."

To the partner who is not on the same page:

"Here is what I've been trying. Here is what has changed."

Lead with outcomes, not theory. Do not hand them the book and say "read this." (That is a demand.) Share one specific change you made and one specific result you observed. "I stopped saying 'get dressed' and started putting clothes on the chair without a word. The morning took fifteen minutes instead of forty-five." Concrete. Observable. Not a framework they have to adopt. A result they can see.

"Can we agree on one thing to try together for one week?"

One shared commitment is more valuable than comprehensive alignment that neither of you can sustain. "We will both use declarative language instead of direct commands." "We will both drop demands when we see the window closing." "Neither of us will use consequences as a response to avoidance." Start there. Build from what works.

To siblings:

"Your sibling's brain works differently, and they need different things to feel safe. That doesn't mean your feelings matter less."

"It's okay to be frustrated about this. You're allowed to feel that way."

"I will never ask you to be the grown-up in this house. That's my job."

"What do you need from me right now? I'm asking because I want to make sure you're okay too."

"You and your sibling are different people. I love you the same, and I parent you the way each of you needs."

To yourself, when someone gives you bad advice:

"They are applying a neurotypical framework. It is right for most children and wrong for mine. I can discard the advice without discarding the person."

You will hear "they just need consequences" a hundred more times. You will hear "you're too soft" at family dinners. You will hear "they'll never learn if you keep accommodating." Having a single internal sentence ready for those moments keeps your own window from narrowing in response to advice that does not apply to your situation.

The plays in action

The phrases above are tools. These vignettes show what it looks like when several of them work together in real time. None of these went perfectly. All of them went better than the alternative.

Morning: the shirt is wrong

It is 7:20 AM. Your child is standing in the hallway holding a shirt and crying. The shirt was fine yesterday. Today it is not fine. You do not know why. They do not know why. You need to leave in twenty-five minutes.

Your body wants to say: "That shirt is fine. Just put it on. We're going to be late." You feel the urgency in your chest.

You check your state. Jaw tight. Shoulders up. You take a breath and drop your shoulders. Three seconds.

You sit down on the hallway floor. Not standing over them. Not between them and their room. Just down.

> "Something about this morning is really hard." (Empathy. Full stop. No "but.")

Silence. They are still holding the shirt and crying.

"You don't have to wear that." (Lower Demands. The shirt is not the priority. Leaving the house in some form of clothing is.)

You wait. Sixty seconds of silence that feels like ten minutes. You say nothing. You do not suggest another shirt. You do not reference the time.

They drop the shirt on the floor and walk back to their room. You do not follow. Two minutes later they come out in yesterday's shirt. You say nothing about it.

> "There's toast on the counter." (Declarative. Offer Without Requiring.)

They eat the toast standing up. You hand them their shoes without a word. They put them on.

You are nine minutes late. Nobody yelled. The relationship is intact. The demand budget has room left for whatever comes next.

Plays used: the 30-second self-check, sitting down, empathy without "but," dropping the demand, declarative language, silence as intervention, Offer Without Requiring.

Meltdown: the homework trigger

Your child agreed to do homework after dinner. Dinner is over. You said "the homework folder is on the table" (declarative, not a command). They walked to the table, opened the folder, looked at the worksheet, and are now on the kitchen floor screaming.

Your instinct: explain that it is only ten problems, offer to help, remind them they agreed to this.

Instead: you sit down in a chair nearby. Not at the table. Not looming. You say: "I'm here. There's no rush." Then you stop talking.

They scream for two more minutes. You breathe. You unclench your jaw. You are not fixing this. You are surviving it without making it worse.

The screaming slows. They are crying now, not screaming. Their body is shifting from rigid to curled.

You wait. Three more minutes of quiet crying. You say nothing. You do not ask "are you okay?" You do not reference the homework.

Their breathing deepens. They sit up. They do not look at you.

> "I'm going to make some tea. Want some?" (Test. Smallest possible next thing. Not the homework.)
>
> "No."

That is useful data. Not yet. You make tea. You sit in the living room. Eight minutes later they come to the couch and sit on the other end.

You do not mention the homework. Twenty minutes later they say, without looking at you: "Can you read me the problems and I just say the answers?"

"Yeah." (Align. They set the terms.)

You scribe. They answer. All ten problems. Twelve minutes. The homework is done.

The meltdown took thirty minutes. The homework took twelve. If you had pushed through the meltdown, the entire evening would have been consumed. The nervous system needed what it needed. The homework happened when the window reopened.

Plays used: declarative language for the original bid, sitting down, "I'm here, there's no rush," silence through the meltdown, waiting past comfort, testing with something tiny, not mentioning the demand, letting them set the terms.

Public: the grocery store

You are in aisle four. Your child was fine in aisles one through three. Something shifted. Maybe the fluorescent lights. Maybe the cumulative sensory load. Maybe the person who walked too close. You do not know. They have stopped walking and their face has gone flat. You recognize shutdown.

The old move: "We're almost done, just two more things." Or: "Do you want to pick a treat?" Or: "Come on, we need to finish."

Instead: "Let's go sit in the car for a bit." (Genuine exit. Not a punishment. Not "if you can't handle it." An exit.)

They do not respond. Shutdown. Language processing is limited.

You leave the cart where it is. You walk toward the exit. You do not hold their hand or guide them unless they reach for you. You walk slowly. They follow, three steps behind.

In the car, you start the engine for air conditioning. You say nothing. You do not turn on music. You do not ask what happened. You sit.

Four minutes of silence. Their shoulders drop. They take a deeper breath.

> "There's water in the cup holder." (Offer Without Requiring. No eye contact demand. No comment on what just happened.)

They drink the water.

Six more minutes. They say: "Can we just go home?"

"Yeah. We can come back another time." (Genuine. No disappointment in your voice. The groceries are not worth more than this.)

You go home. The groceries wait. Nobody was lectured. Nobody was shamed. The car was the retreat space and it worked.

Plays used: reading shutdown, genuine exit offer, leaving the cart, slow pace, silence in the car, Offer Without Requiring, no processing of the event, accepting the "go home" without resistance.

Wanting but not being able: the birthday party

Your child was invited to a birthday party. They want to go. They talked about it for three days. They picked out a gift. They got dressed. They are now sitting on the stairs and will not get in the car.

Every part of you wants to say: "But you want to go! You've been excited all week!" You want to gently push them to the car because you know, from experience, that sometimes once they get there they are fine.

But you also know that when the push fails, the meltdown happens at the party, far from home, with an audience.

You sit on the stairs. Not blocking them. Not positioned toward the door. Just near.

"It's okay to want something and not be able to do it right now. Those are two different things." (The key sentence for this scenario. Names exactly what they are experiencing.)

They do not respond. Their jaw is tight. They are staring at the floor.

"The option is there if you want it. No pressure either way." (Genuine. You have to mean the "no pressure" part. If your body is angled toward the door, they will read it.)

You wait. Two minutes.

"What if we just drive past and you can decide in the car?" (Align. Offer a smaller version. Genuine only if "no" in the car is actually available.)

"What if I hate it?"

"Then we leave. Your call on timing. Whenever you say go, we go."

They get in the car. You drive. They decide at the end of the street to go in. They stay for forty minutes and then text you: "Come get me." You come. No commentary on the timing.

In the car on the way home: "The cake was good." That is all they say. That is a connection bid. You respond: "Good." Nothing more. The bid was low-energy. Your response matches.

Plays used: sitting down, the "two different things" sentence, genuine no-pressure offer, offering a smaller version, giving explicit exit permission, honoring the exit without commentary, matching the energy of their connection bid.

Bedtime: the routine that is not a routine

It is 8:00 PM. Your child's window has been narrowing since dinner. You can see it in their posture, their short answers, the way they are curled into the couch. The demand budget is nearly empty.

The old routine: pajamas, teeth, book, bed. Four demands delivered in sequence.

Tonight: you lower the lights in the living room without announcing it. (Environment. No verbal demand.) You place a glass of water on the side table. (Offer Without Requiring.) You say: "I'm heading to bed soon. Goodnight when you're ready." (Declarative. Time information without time pressure. No specific demand.)

You go to the kitchen. You do not hover. You do not check on them. You load the dishwasher, which is a sound they associate with the end of the evening. Predictable. (Environment. Shared Rhythm through ambient routine.)

Twenty minutes later you hear movement. They have gone to their room. You did not tell them to. The environmental cues and the absence of demands let the transition happen on their own terms.

You walk past their door. It is open. You say: "Night." One word. No hug demand. No teeth reminder. No tucking in sequence.

"Night."

They are in bed in yesterday's clothes. The teeth are unbrushed. Nobody cried. Nobody fought. Sleep will come. The teeth will happen tomorrow when the window is wider.

Plays used: environmental demand reduction (lights), Offer Without Requiring (water), declarative language with no time pressure, ambient routine as Shared Rhythm, one-word exchange, releasing the performance of bedtime.

Using this chapter

This chapter is a reference. It is not meant to be read once and absorbed. It is meant to be returned to. The morning is falling apart: flip to "When the morning is falling apart." They refused the birthday party: flip to "When they refuse something they want to do." You lost your temper: flip to "When you have lost your temper."

The printable version of the key phrases from this chapter is in the Appendix. Print it. Cut it apart. Put the sections where you will see them when you need them: on the fridge, inside a cabinet door, taped to the bathroom mirror, tucked into your phone case.

PART FOUR

Your Nervous System Is Part of This

PART FOUR

Chapter 12: Your Nervous System Is Part of This

You have the framework. You have the crisis protocol. You have the scenarios and the playbook. You know what demand sensitivity is, how the three mechanisms work, and what your child's nervous system needs from the environment around it.

Now we turn the lens on you. Not because you are the problem. Because you are the lever.

Of all the variables in your child's life (the school system, the sensory environment, the social world, the institutional demands, the broader culture) you are the one you have the most control over. You cannot redesign the school by next week. You cannot rewire your child's threat-detection circuitry. But you can change what your child's nervous system encounters when it encounters you. And what it encounters when it encounters you is one of the most powerful variables in the equation.

This part of the book exists because of co-regulation. Chapter 7 introduced the mechanism: your nervous system and your child's are in constant communication through channels that operate below conscious awareness. Your state influences their state. Not sometimes. Constantly. When you are regulated, the environment your child encounters is different from when you are activated. The strategies are the same. The person delivering them is different. And the person delivering them is what the child's nervous system reads first.

A dysregulated parent implementing a perfect framework is still transmitting dysregulation.

That sentence is not meant to add pressure. It is meant to clarify why the next four chapters matter. If the framework is the tool, your nervous system is the delivery system. A good tool in a shaky hand works less well than the same tool in a steady one. The next four chapters are about steadying the hand. Not to be perfect. Not to be calm all the time. That is not realistic and expecting it of yourself is another demand on a system that already has too many. But to notice your state, to understand what depletes it, to recognize the patterns that pull you out of your window, and to repair when you get it wrong. That is the work.

You are the tuning fork

Chapter 7 used this metaphor briefly. It deserves more room here because it is the single most useful image for understanding why your regulation matters.

Two tuning forks. Strike one and place it near the other. The second fork starts vibrating at the same frequency without being touched. Nobody touched it. Nobody told it to vibrate. The physics of proximity did the work.

Your nervous system is the first tuning fork. Your child's is the second.

When your fork is vibrating with anxiety (the morning is running late, the school called again, the in-laws are coming this weekend, the bills are due), your child's system encounters that vibration. It does not know the source. It does not know the content. It reads the frequency: activated. And it adjusts its own state in the direction of activated.

When your fork is vibrating with urgency (we have to go, we need to get through this, I need them to cooperate right now), the frequency your child encounters is pressure. Pressure is a demand. Their threat-detection system reads it as such and responds accordingly: avoidance, resistance, shutdown, meltdown. Not because of what you said. Because of what your body was broadcasting while you said it.

When your fork is relatively steady (present, unhurried, not transmitting agenda) your child's system encounters something different. It encounters a frequency that is not demanding a response. It encounters a person whose body is communicating: nothing is urgent right now. There is room here. That encounter does not guarantee that your child will regulate. But it creates the conditions in which regulation is possible. A steady tuning fork near an activated one does not force the activated fork to match it. It offers a frequency the activated fork can entrain to. The offer is constant. Whether it is received in this moment or the next moment or tomorrow is up to the other system.

This is why the framework works better on some days than others even when you do everything the same. On the days it works best, your state was probably steadier. On the days it fell apart, your state was probably activated before the interaction started. Not because you did something wrong. Because you are a person living inside a high-demand situation and your nervous system has its own budget that depletes and replenishes the same way your child's does.

The 30-second question

Here is a practical tool you can use before any interaction.

Before you walk into the morning routine. Before you address the homework. Before you respond to the meltdown. Before you open the door to their room. Before you attempt a transition that you know will be difficult. Ask yourself one question:

Will this go better if I take 30 seconds first?

That is it. Not: should I regulate? Not: am I being a good enough parent? Not: what is my nervous system state on a scale of one to ten? Just: will the next ten minutes cost me more or less if I walk in like this?

If you check in with your body and you are in your window (thinking clearly, present, flexible, not carrying tension from the last interaction or the last hour) then go. Handle it. You have the capacity right now and spending time on regulation you do not need is itself a demand on your time and your attention.

If you check in and you are outside your window (activated: tense, irritable, racing thoughts, urgency in your chest, jaw tight. Or shutdown: numb, flat, going through the motions, checked out) the math changes. You already know what happens when you engage from that state. The interaction escalates. Your child's system reads yours and responds in kind. The thing that was going to take ten minutes takes forty-five. You end up in a repair cycle that costs more than the thirty seconds would have.

Thirty seconds. Breathe. Unclench your jaw. Drop your shoulders. Feel your feet on the floor. Name your state out loud if you can: "I'm activated right now." That naming alone creates a small separation between you and the state. You are not the activation. You are the person noticing the activation. That separation gives you a sliver of choice about what happens next.

Sometimes the situation will not wait. The child is already escalated. Something is unsafe. The bus is here and there is no margin. In those moments, you skip the thirty seconds and you do the best you can from wherever you are. That answer is honest too. The question is not "did I regulate perfectly before every interaction?" The question is "did I check, and when I had thirty seconds, did I use them?"

Over time, the check becomes automatic. You will start to notice your state without being asked to notice it. You will feel the jaw tightening before you walk into the room and you will pause without having to think about whether to pause. That automaticity is the skill. Not perfection. Awareness.

What changes when you change

When a parent becomes more regulated, more attuned, and less demand-generating, specific things shift in the dynamic. Not abstract things. Observable things.

The demand load decreases. When you are aware of the demands you are placing (explicit, implicit, and invisible) you place fewer of them. You catch the fourth ask before it leaves your mouth. You notice the urgency in your posture and slow down. You hear the "but" forming after your empathic statement and you stop before it lands. Each of these small reductions lowers the total demand your child's nervous system encounters in a given day.

The relational environment becomes more predictable. When your child can predict what you will do, because you respond from regulation rather than reacting from whatever state you happen to be in, uncertainty-driven activation decreases. Your child's nervous system spends less energy scanning you for threat because you have become a known quantity. That energy is freed up for other things: tolerating a demand, engaging with a task, being in a relationship.

Rupture-and-repair cycles get shorter. You will still get it wrong. You will still yell, push too hard, or revert to old patterns. That is not going to stop. What changes is the speed of recognition. The gap between the rupture and the moment you realize what happened gets shorter. And as it gets shorter, the repair comes sooner. The cycles tighten. The damage per cycle decreases. The relationship absorbs the ruptures more easily because the account has more in it.

Your child stops spending energy managing your responses. This one is invisible but significant. Right now, a portion of your child's cognitive and physiological resources is going toward tracking your state. Are you upset? Are you about to place another demand? Is this about to escalate? Are you disappointed? Are you pretending to be okay? That tracking is constant and it is expensive. It draws from the same demand budget as everything else. When your state becomes more regulated and more predictable, those resources are freed. Your child has more window available, not because you fixed their nervous system, but because you stopped being a variable that depleted it.

None of this happens immediately. None of it happens in a straight line. The progress looks like two steps forward and one step back, for months, until you look back at where you started and realize that the baseline has shifted. The mornings are not perfect. But the average morning is different from the average morning six months ago. That is the trajectory. Not perfection. Shift.

This is leverage, not guilt

You will read this chapter and feel guilty. Almost every parent does. The thought process goes: if my state affects my child's nervous system, and my child is struggling, then my dysregulation is contributing to their struggle, which means I am part of the problem, which means I need to be better, which means I am failing.

That thought process is a demand spiral. Each step adds another demand on your system. By the end of it you are more activated than when you started, which is the opposite of what this chapter is asking for.

So let us be direct about what this chapter is saying and what it is not saying.

It is saying: your state is a variable. It is one of many variables. You did not cause your child's demand sensitivity. Your dysregulation did not create their nervous system profile. Their PDA would exist regardless of your state. You are not the cause.

It is also saying: of all the variables in the equation, you are the one most responsive to change. You cannot change the school. You cannot change the sensory world. You cannot change the diagnostic landscape or the shortage of PDA-informed professionals or the extended family members who think your child needs firmer limits. But you can change, gradually, over time, what your child's nervous system encounters when it encounters you. That is not guilt. That is the most empowering piece of information in this entire book.

You are not the problem. You are the most powerful lever available. The distinction matters. A problem is something to be fixed. A lever is something to be used. You do not need to fix yourself. You need to understand that your state has influence, and that influence can be pointed in a helpful direction.

PART FOUR

Chapter 13: Your Burnout Is Real

You are tired in a way that sleep does not fix.

This is not the tiredness of a hard week at work. It is not the tiredness of new parenthood, which is brutal but bounded. People told you it would get easier. It did not get easier. It changed shape. The demands shifted from the physical exhaustion of early childhood to the psychological exhaustion of managing a nervous system crisis that has been running for years. The sleep deprivation gave way to something worse: chronic depletion of your capacity to regulate, to connect, to think clearly, to be the person you want to be in the room with your child.

Burnout in PDA parenting is not a character flaw. It is not a sign that you are not resilient enough, not committed enough, not trying hard enough. It is the predictable result of chronic demand overload on your own nervous system. The same mechanism that operates in your child operates in you. Your system has a demand budget. Your system depletes through use and replenishes through recovery. And the demands on your system have been exceeding the recovery for a long time.

You are running a deficit. This chapter is about seeing it clearly and starting to address it. Not with self-care advice that adds another demand to your list. With an honest look at what is actually depleting you and what would actually help.

The burnout you are carrying

PDA parenting burnout is different from general parenting burnout because the stressor is different. General parenting burnout comes from the volume and repetition of ordinary demands: the laundry, the meals, the logistics, the scheduling, the endless management of a household. PDA parenting burnout comes from something additional: the sustained experience of living alongside a nervous system that processes ordinary life as threatening.

Your system absorbs that, day after day. You wake up and your first thought is about what today will cost. You calculate demand loads before breakfast. You read your child's posture when they come downstairs and your own nervous system adjusts before they have said a word. You are hypervigilant in your own home, scanning for the shift that signals the window is closing. You are performing regulation while your own system is screaming for rest. You are managing a crisis that looks invisible to the outside world, which means you are doing it without the support or acknowledgment that visible crises receive.

The hypervigilance alone is exhausting. Monitoring another person's nervous system state in real time, all day, while managing your own state, while managing the household, while managing the other children, while managing the school communications, while managing the extended family's opinions, while managing your own grief about how different this is from what you expected. That is not a sustainable workload. The fact that you have been sustaining it does not mean it is sustainable. It means you have been running on fumes and calling it functioning.

Check in with yourself right now. Not as a test. As a map.

Are you activated? Tense, irritable, racing thoughts, urgency running in the background even when nothing urgent is happening. Difficulty sitting still. Short fuse. Startling easily. Jaw clenched more often than not.

Are you in your window? Thinking clearly. Present. Able to be flexible. Able to feel something other than anxiety or exhaustion.

Are you in shutdown? Numb. Flat. Going through the motions. Not fully here. Doing what needs to be done without feeling much about any of it. Unable to access joy even when something good happens. Checked out in ways you may not have noticed because checked out has become your normal.

Most PDA parents reading this will land in activated or shutdown. If you landed in your window, good. Protect that. If you landed outside it, that is the information this chapter is built to address.

Your demand audit

Chapter 8 taught you to audit your child's demand load. This chapter asks you to audit your own.

Look at a typical week. Not an ideal week. A real one. Write down everything you do, everything you are expected to do, and everything you expect of yourself. Not just the big things. The small ones count.

The texts you feel obligated to return within the hour. The laundry standard you are holding. The meal expectations. The social commitments you dread but keep. The work responsibilities that have not been adjusted despite everything else that has changed. The volunteer work you said yes to before you knew what this year would look like. The house standard you maintain because letting it go feels like losing control of the one thing you can control. The emotional labor of managing everyone else's feelings about your child's situation. The invisible work of researching PDA, reading books, finding providers, filling out forms, writing emails to the school.

Write it all down. Then ask three questions about each one.

Did I choose this, or did it just accumulate? Many of the demands in your life were never consciously chosen. They drifted in. The obligation to host Thanksgiving. The commitment to the school fundraiser. The standard of clean that was set when your life looked different. Recognizing that you picked something up without choosing it is the first step toward recognizing you can set it down.

What would actually happen if I lowered this? Not what feels like it would happen. What would actually happen. The house is messier. The meals are simpler. You skip book club for a month. You say no to Thanksgiving hosting this year. You let the emails wait twenty-four hours instead of responding immediately. For most items on the list, the honest answer is: nothing catastrophic. The world adjusts. People adapt. The standard was yours, not the universe's.

Is this demand serving my family right now, or is it serving a version of my life that no longer exists? Some of what you carry made sense before PDA parenting filled the capacity it fills. It may not make sense anymore. The career ambition that assumed you would have evenings free. The social life that assumed weekends were available. The body of volunteer work that assumed surplus energy. Those assumptions belonged to a different life. Carrying the demands of that life into this one is not dedication. It is a failure to triage, and triage is exactly what this situation requires.

The full Personal Demand Audit worksheet is in the Appendix (Tool 2). Completing it once will change what you see.

Not every parent has equal room to make these choices. A single parent working two jobs does not have the same flexibility as a two-parent household with financial margin. Economic pressure, cultural expectations, systemic demands: all of these constrain what you can actually release. If most of your demands are genuinely non-negotiable, that is important data about how much support you need, not evidence that you should be handling this alone. If you cannot lower the demands, you need to increase the support. Both are valid responses to an overloaded system.

For the demands that are negotiable, that you have been carrying out of habit or identity or obligation rather than genuine necessity: those are the ones worth examining. Releasing even one creates space. Space is what you are missing. Space is what allows you to be the lever the framework needs you to be.

The demands you did not choose and cannot see

The personal demand audit captures the things you do and the things you are expected to do. But there is another category of demand on your system that the audit does not capture because you did not choose it and may not have identified it.

Your phone.

Every notification is a demand on your nervous system. A sensory demand (the buzz, the sound, the screen lighting up). An attention demand (what is it? should I check?). And if you check, a content demand: the news is designed to activate your threat system. Social media is designed to generate engagement through emotional activation. The Instagram feed of families who seem to be doing this without breaking is placing a comparison demand on you that registers below conscious awareness. The PDA parent group where someone is always in crisis is placing an empathy demand on you that you absorb because their crisis looks like yours. The group chat that pings forty times before lunch is a sustained interruption demand that fragments your attention all morning.

Each of these is a withdrawal from your demand budget. Not the kind you chose. Not the kind that shows up on a to-do list. But your nervous system processes them the same way it processes any other demand: as something requiring a response.

The mechanism is identical to what happens in your child. Every demand is a withdrawal from the budget. When the budget is depleted, even small things produce large responses. If you have ever snapped at your child after twenty minutes of reading the news, that was not a parenting failure. That was a depleted budget producing the only response it had left.

This is not a lecture about screen time for adults. You are an adult and you get to make your own choices about how you use your phone. But the demand audit applies to the information environment the same way it applies to everything else. You are looking for demands you can lower so that the capacity you already have can be pointed where it is needed most.

Some things that reduce the load, not because they are virtuous but because the mechanism supports them. The first hour of the morning matters most. If the first thing you encounter is your phone, your nervous system starts the day processing demands before your feet hit the floor. The news will still be there at 8 AM. Your window will be wider if you reach it on your own terms. Notifications are demands. Turning off the non-essential ones means you choose when to engage instead of your phone choosing for you. Social media comparison is an invisible demand. The parent on Instagram whose child is thriving, whose house is clean, whose family went on vacation and looked happy: that image is placing a demand on you. The demand is: you should be doing better. You do not have to delete the apps. But noticing what they cost you is part of the audit.

You do not have to overhaul your digital life. You need to see it as part of your demand landscape and make intentional choices about what stays, what gets reduced, and what gets set aside. The same three questions from the demand audit apply: did I choose this? What would happen if I lowered it? Is it serving my family right now?

What you actually need

Most self-care advice for parents is useless. Take a bath. Light a candle. Do yoga. Schedule a date night. These recommendations assume that what you are experiencing is ordinary stress that responds to ordinary relaxation. What you are experiencing is not ordinary stress. It is the sustained depletion of your nervous system's capacity to regulate in the context of a chronic, largely invisible crisis. A bath does not fix that. Pretending it does just adds one more demand: the demand to feel better after doing the thing that was supposed to make you feel better.

What you actually need:

Another regulated adult who understands. Not someone who listens politely and then says "have you tried being more consistent?" Not someone who nods and then changes the subject to their own parenting struggles which are real but are not this. Someone who knows what PDA is. Someone whose nervous system does not add to your load when you are with them. Someone you do not have to translate for before you can feel heard. This might be a partner, a friend, a therapist, another PDA parent, an online community. But you need at least one person who gets it without requiring you to justify your approach before you can exhale.

Genuine respite. Not respite that is contingent on your child being "manageable" for whoever watches them. Not respite that comes with a debrief about everything that went wrong while you were gone. Not respite where you are on call by text, managing the situation remotely, bracing for what you will walk back into. Respite that is genuinely free. Where you are unreachable. Where no one is waiting for your instructions. Where you can set your nervous system down for a few hours and not pick it up again until you are ready. This is extraordinarily hard to arrange with a demand sensitive child. It is also non-negotiable for long-term sustainability. You cannot pour from an empty bucket. That sentence is a cliche because it is true.

Permission to grieve. Chapter 6 named it. The grief does not resolve. It comes back. You need spaces where it is allowed to come back without being redirected toward gratitude or silver linings. A therapist who can hold the complexity of your situation without requiring you to reach acceptance is one of the most valuable supports available. Not to fix you. To give your nervous system a space where it is the one being attended to, for once, instead of the one doing all the attending.

Professional support for you. If your burnout is persistent (more days outside your window than in it, most weeks, for months) you need your own clinical support. Not to learn more parenting strategies. Not to process your child's diagnosis. To have a space where someone is tracking your nervous system state with the same care you are giving to your child's. Find a therapist who understands neurodivergence and the demands of PDA parenting. Share this book with them. It will save you weeks of explaining.

If you want support from clinicians trained in the RELATE framework specifically, consultations are available at relatepda.com.

One demand you can release this week

You do not need to overhaul your life tonight. You need to make room. Even a small amount of room changes what is possible.

Look at the demands you identified. The ones you did not choose. The ones that are serving a version of your life that no longer exists. The ones where the honest answer to "what would actually happen?" is: nothing bad.

Pick one. Release it this week. Not forever. For now. See what the room feels like.

That room is the space in which the lever works. Without it, you are implementing a framework from depletion. With it, you have something left to bring into the room with your child. Something that is not urgency. Something that is not exhaustion. Something their nervous system will read as: this person has capacity right now. This person is not running on empty.

That reading changes everything that follows.

PART FOUR

Chapter 14: Your Patterns

You cannot reduce what you have not identified.

Chapter 8 taught you to audit the demands on your child. Chapter 13 taught you to audit the demands on yourself. This chapter holds up a mirror to something more specific: the patterns you fall into when you are interacting with your child. Not the demands themselves. The sequences. The loops. The habits so deeply wired that you are in the middle of one before you realize it has started.

These are not character flaws. They are deeply ingrained habits shaped by how most of us were parented and what the culture tells us good parenting looks like. You did not choose them. You absorbed them. They are in your muscle memory. They live in your vocal cords and your posture and the way your body orients toward your child when you need something to happen.

Recognizing them is not about guilt. It is about having accurate data on what your child's nervous system is actually encountering every day. The demand audit from Chapter 8 counts the demands. This chapter identifies the delivery system.

The compliance loop

You make a request. They resist. You repeat the request, a little louder or a little firmer. They escalate. You escalate. They escalate further. The interaction ends in a meltdown or a shutdown, and you are left standing in the kitchen wondering what just happened.

What happened is the loop itself.

Each repetition of the demand doubled the demand load. The first ask was one demand. The second ask was two: the original demand plus the implicit demand of "I already asked you once." The third ask was three: the original, the repetition, and the escalating frustration in your voice that communicates "I am losing patience and something is about to change." By the third ask, your child's nervous system was managing not just the original request but the escalating threat of your activation.

The compliance loop is the most common pattern in PDA parenting because it is the most natural thing in the world. You need something to happen. It is not happening. You ask again. The asking again feels like the obvious response. It is the obvious response for a child whose thinking brain is online and who is choosing not to comply. For a child whose threat-detection system has already activated, asking again is pouring fuel on a fire.

What the loop looks like from the outside: a parent getting progressively more frustrated over something that should be simple.

What the loop looks like from inside the child's nervous system: the threat is getting louder. The demand is getting heavier. The person delivering the demand is becoming less safe. Each repetition confirms that this person will not stop until I comply or collapse.

How to break it: one ask. Then wait. If the ask does not produce movement, the window is not open enough for that demand right now. Either lower the demand, change the delivery, or come back later. Do not repeat. Repetition is escalation dressed as patience.

This is the hardest pattern to break because it operates below conscious awareness. You will find yourself on the third ask before you realize you have asked three times. The progress is not in never entering the loop. It is in recognizing you are in it sooner. The gap between the first ask and the recognition that you are repeating yourself gets shorter. That shortening is the skill.

The capacity assumption

"But they did it yesterday."

This thought drives more demand-placing than any other single pattern. It sounds reasonable. It sounds like evidence. They demonstrated capacity yesterday. The demand is the same. Therefore they should be able to do it today. The logic is clean.

The logic is wrong.

Yesterday's nervous system state is not today's nervous system state. The window of tolerance varies based on sleep, demand load, sensory state, what happened at school, what happened in the hour before you asked, what happened in the five minutes before you asked, and variables you cannot see and they may not be able to name. Monday's capacity is data about Monday. It is not a prediction about Tuesday.

The capacity assumption is damaging because it is not just a thought you have. It is a thought that leaks. It leaks into the way you ask: a little more firmly, because you know they can do this. It leaks into your posture: a little more expectant, because yesterday proved it is possible. It leaks into your frustration when they cannot do it: faster, hotter, because this is not about the demand being too hard, this is about them not doing something you know they can do. The child's nervous system reads all of that. It reads: this person believes I am choosing not to do this. This person thinks I am capable and refusing. That reading is a relational threat on top of the demand threat. Two threats, one interaction.

The counter-pattern: every day is a fresh read. Before you present a demand, read the window. Not yesterday's window. Today's. Right now. What does their posture tell you? Their face? Their voice? Their energy? That data is more relevant than what happened twenty-four hours ago.

If you catch yourself thinking "but they did it yesterday," that thought is a signal. Not a signal about their capacity. A signal that you are about to place a demand based on outdated data. Update the data. Read the window. Respond to what is in front of you.

The empathy-demand sequence

"I know this is hard, but we still need to get dressed."

You learned this somewhere. A book, a therapist, a parenting class. Lead with empathy. Validate the feeling. Then redirect to the expectation. It sounds compassionate. It sounds like you are meeting them where they are and then guiding them forward.

Their nervous system hears something different.

Their nervous system hears the empathy and registers: this person sees that I am struggling. For a fraction of a second, the system detects safety. Someone sees me. Then the "but" arrives. And the demand lands. The safety signal is replaced instantly by a demand signal. The nervous system learns, through repetition: when this person validates my experience, a demand is coming next. The empathy is not genuine attunement. It is the windup before the pitch.

Over time, this pattern teaches your child to stop trusting your empathic openings. They hear "I know this is hard" and they brace. The words that were supposed to communicate understanding now communicate incoming pressure. The empathy has been colonized by the demand, the same way an interest can be colonized by using it as a bridge too many times.

The fix is simple to describe and difficult to execute. Empathy without a "but." "This morning feels really hard." Full stop. Silence. Wait. The empathy is the complete statement. What comes next is determined by the child's response, not by your agenda.

If you cannot do this because the demand genuinely needs to happen, at minimum separate the empathy from the demand by time and space. Empathy now. Walk away. Come back in five minutes with the demand, delivered differently. The separation prevents the pairing. The child's nervous system gets to experience the empathy as genuine because the demand did not arrive in the same breath.

Listen to yourself for one day. Count how many times the word "but" appears after an empathic statement. The number will be higher than you think. Each one is a paired association being deposited into your child's nervous system: empathy means a demand is coming.

The disguised demand

"Would you like to take a shower?"

Only "yes" is an acceptable answer.

"Do you want to come help me with dinner?"

Refusal will be met with disappointment or a consequence.

"Don't you think it would be a good idea to start your homework?"

The question is not a question. It is a demand wearing a question's clothing.

Your child's nervous system detects these instantly. Their threat-detection system is designed to identify constraint disguised as choice. That is not a flaw. That is the system operating exactly as it was built to operate. A disguised demand is actually higher-threat than a direct demand because it adds a layer of deception. The direct demand says "put your shoes on." The disguised demand says "would you like to put your shoes on?" and both the parent and the child know that "no" is not an available answer. The child's nervous system now has to process the demand itself plus the dishonesty of the framing. Two threats instead of one.

This does not mean all questions are demands. "Do you want peanut butter or jelly?" is a genuine question if both answers are truly acceptable. "Would you like to come with me or stay here?" is genuine if staying is a real option with no consequences attached. The test is always the same: what happens if they say no? If no produces disappointment, frustration, consequences, or a different demand, the original question was not genuine. It was a demand with a question mark glued to the end.

The alternative is honesty. If something needs to happen, say so directly, using declarative language. "The shower is ready" is more honest and less demand-heavy than "would you like to take a shower?" The declarative statement does not pretend to offer choice it is not offering. It places information in the environment and lets the child's nervous system decide how to respond. Honesty, paradoxically, is less threatening than false choice, because the nervous system does not have to decode it.

Time urgency as demand

"We need to leave in five minutes."

"Hurry up."

"We're going to be late."

"Come on, let's go."

Every reference to the clock is a demand. You know this from Chapter 8. But time urgency as a pattern goes beyond individual sentences. It is a posture. It is a way of moving through the morning. It is the pace of your feet on the floor and the quality of your attention and the way your body leans forward toward the door when it is time to leave. Your child reads all of it. They read the pace before they hear the words.

Time urgency is particularly insidious because it feels justified. You are not making up the deadline. The bus is real. The appointment is real. The school start time is real. The urgency feels like a fact about the world, not a demand you are placing. But to the child's nervous system, the source of the urgency is irrelevant. It registers as threat regardless of whether the threat is manufactured or real. The bus being real does not make the threat response any less activated.

The pattern looks like this: you know you need to leave at 8:15. At 7:45, you start monitoring the clock. Your body subtly shifts. Your movements get faster. Your voice gets clipped. You start referencing time, directly or indirectly. Your child's nervous system reads the shift before you have said a word. Their window begins to narrow, not because of a demand you placed, but because of the urgency your body is broadcasting. By the time you say "we need to go," their system has already been in activation for fifteen minutes, responding to the frequency of your anxiety about time.

The counter-pattern from Chapter 8 applies here: add time or remove demands, never add speed. But the deeper work is noticing when the urgency arrives in your body. Not when you say "hurry up." When your posture changes. When your pace increases. When your attention shifts from your child to the clock. That is when the demand starts transmitting, long before it becomes a sentence.

If you can catch the urgency in your body before it reaches your voice, you can choose to slow your body down even while the clock is real. Walk slower. Breathe. Unclench your jaw. The clock does not change. But what your child's nervous system encounters in the next ten minutes is different, and that difference is the difference between a morning that works and a morning that ends in crisis.

The pattern underneath the patterns

There is a thread running through all five of these patterns. In every case, the parent's internal state is driving the demand before the demand becomes a sentence. The compliance loop is fueled by frustration. The capacity assumption is fueled by expectation. The empathy-demand sequence is fueled by agenda. The disguised demand is fueled by the need for compliance without confrontation. Time urgency is fueled by anxiety about the clock.

In every case, the child's nervous system is reading the fuel, not the sentence.

This is why changing the words is not enough. You can switch to declarative language and still transmit urgency. You can eliminate the "but" after empathy and still carry the agenda in your posture. You can stop referencing the clock and still broadcast time pressure through the pace of your movements. The words are the surface. The state is the signal.

The work of this chapter is not learning new scripts. It is learning to recognize what your nervous system is doing before it reaches your child. Not to judge it. Not to suppress it. To notice it, so that you have a moment of choice between the state and the behavior.

That moment of choice is the gap the 30-second question from Chapter 12 is designed to create. Am I activated right now? Is this going to go better if I take thirty seconds? The patterns described in this chapter are what happen when the answer was yes and you did not take the thirty seconds. The more you recognize the patterns, the more you recognize the moments where thirty seconds would have changed the outcome.

You will not catch every pattern every time. You will be in the compliance loop at 7:45 AM tomorrow. You will catch the capacity assumption after you have already said "but you did it yesterday." You will hear the "but" leave your mouth in the middle of the empathy-demand sequence. The progress is not in eliminating the patterns. It is in shortening the gap between doing the pattern and recognizing you did it. That gap shrinks over weeks and months. The patterns get quieter. They do not disappear. They get quieter.

And when you do catch one in real time, when you feel the third ask forming and you stop, when you notice the urgency in your body and you slow down, when you hear the "but" approaching and you close your mouth instead: that is the lever working. That is your nervous system, slightly more aware than it was last month, producing a different environment for your child. That difference is what changes things. Not all at once. Over time.

PART FOUR

Chapter 15: Repair and (Re)Pair

You are going to get this wrong.

Not once. Repeatedly. You are going to yell when you know you should not. You are going to push a demand past the point where pushing made sense. You are going to fall into the compliance loop at 7:42 AM despite having read the chapter about it twice. You are going to catch the empathy-demand sequence after the "but" has already left your mouth. You are going to feel the urgency rising in your body and watch yourself escalate anyway, fully aware of what you are doing and unable to stop it in time.

This is not failure. This is the reality of rewiring patterns that took years to develop. They will not rewire in a week or a month. What changes is the speed of recognition. The gap between the rupture and the moment you realize what happened gets shorter. As it gets shorter, the repair comes sooner. And the repair is what matters.

Ruptures do not destroy the relationship. Absence of repair does.

Every time.

What repair looks like with a demand sensitive child

Repair with a PDA child is different from repair with most children because the repair itself carries demand. "I'm sorry I yelled" requires them to receive your words, process the apology, evaluate its sincerity, manage whatever feelings the original rupture stirred up, and generate some kind of response. That is five demands inside a two-sentence apology.

If the window is closed when you attempt the repair, the repair becomes another demand on a system that is already past capacity. You are asking them to do work (receive, process, evaluate, feel, respond) at a moment when they cannot do work. The repair does not land. It bounces off. Or worse, it becomes another source of threat: this person is now requiring me to engage with their feelings about what they did to me.

This means repair with a demand sensitive child follows different rules than repair with most people. The rules are not complicated. They are counterintuitive.

It is on their timeline, not yours. You may feel the urge to repair immediately. The tension is uncomfortable. The guilt is uncomfortable. You want to make it right, and making it right means saying the words and receiving some signal that the relationship is okay. That urge is about your discomfort, not their readiness. If they are still activated or shut down, the repair is a demand. Wait. The timing belongs to their nervous system, not your guilt.

Sometimes repair happens thirty minutes later. Sometimes it happens the next day. Sometimes it happens three days later. The delay does not mean the repair will not land. It means the window was not open enough to receive it yet. Your job during the delay is to remain available without pursuing. Do not withdraw into your own guilt and become emotionally unavailable. Do not hover and ask "can we talk about earlier?" every hour. Be present. Be warm. Be reachable. Wait.

It does not require their participation. "I'm sorry I yelled earlier. You don't need to say anything about it." That is repair. It is complete. The child does not need to respond. They do not need to say "it's okay." They do not need to forgive you. They do not need to make eye contact. The repair is something you offer. It is not a transaction that requires a receipt.

"I'm sorry I yelled, are we okay?" is not repair. It is a demand for reassurance dressed as repair. The child now has to manage your need to know the relationship survived, on top of whatever they are still carrying from the rupture itself. Drop the question. Offer the repair. Walk away. Let it sit.

Your child may acknowledge it. They may ignore it. They may test it by repeating the exact behavior that triggered the original rupture, to see if the repair was real or conditional. None of those responses mean the repair did not land. The nervous system heard it. What it does with it is not yours to manage.

It is specific, not general. "I'm sorry I pushed you about getting dressed this morning. That was too much pressure and I can see that now." That names what happened and owns it. The child's nervous system hears: this person understands specifically what went wrong. That specificity communicates genuine awareness. It is evidence that you actually saw what happened, not merely that you noticed tension.

"I'm sorry about earlier" is vague enough to be dismissed by a system that has learned to be skeptical of apologies. Vague apologies cost nothing to produce and communicate nothing about whether you understand what happened. Specific apologies cost more to produce and communicate everything.

It does not include "but." "I'm sorry I yelled, but you weren't listening" is not repair. The "but" redirects responsibility to the child. Their nervous system hears the full message: the apology was conditional, and the real conclusion is that this was still your fault. Repair with a justification attached is a demand wrapped in an apology. If you have a "but" forming after your apology, close your mouth. The "but" is your nervous system's attempt to distribute the blame. That distribution may be emotionally accurate (maybe they were not listening, maybe the situation was genuinely frustrating) but it does not belong in the repair. The repair is your part. Their part is theirs. Mixing them together cancels the repair.

Forced apologies from the child are demands, not repair. If your child apologizes on their own, in their own time, in their own way, that is meaningful. It came from them. If you require it ("you need to say sorry too") you are teaching them that repair is a performance. Words you produce to satisfy someone else's need for closure. That is not what repair is. Let their repair come from them. It may not look like the word "sorry." It may look like sitting closer to you. Making you a cup of tea. Showing you something on their screen. Starting a conversation as if nothing happened. Each of these can be repair, delivered in the language their nervous system can manage.

You will repair the same patterns repeatedly

This is the part that can feel discouraging, so it is worth naming directly.

You will find yourself repairing the same ruptures, caused by the same patterns, more than once. You will recognize the compliance loop in the middle of doing it again. You will catch the empathy-demand sequence after it has landed. You will feel the frustration rise and watch yourself escalate despite everything you know.

This is normal. Your patterns took years to develop. They are wired into your nervous system the same way your child's threat response is wired into theirs. You cannot unwire years of conditioning in a month. What you can do is tighten the cycle. The first time you catch a pattern, it might be hours later, lying in bed, replaying the morning. The tenth time, you catch it in the car on the way to school. The fiftieth time, you catch it in the middle of the sentence. The hundredth time, you feel it forming and you stop before it starts.

That progression is real progress. It does not look dramatic. It does not feel like transformation. But the gap between the pattern firing and your awareness of it is the single most important variable in your growth as a PDA parent. As that gap shrinks, the repair comes sooner, the ruptures get smaller, and the relationship accumulates more evidence that it can survive conflict.

Verbal repair followed by behavioral repetition is not repair. If you apologize for yelling on Monday and yell again on Tuesday, the Monday apology starts to lose weight. Not immediately. Not after one repetition. But over time, if the words do not match the behavior, the child's nervous system learns that apologies are sounds, not signals. The real repair is changed behavior over time. The words are the beginning. The behavior is the proof. And the behavior changes slowly, in the way described above: tightening cycles, shortening gaps, catching it sooner. That slow change is the proof your child's nervous system is tracking.

(Re)Pair: when words are not the way in

Everything above is about verbal repair. What to say, how to say it, what not to say. And that matters. But for many demand sensitive children, verbal repair is itself a demand. "I'm sorry I yelled" requires them to receive language, process meaning, manage emotion, and decide how to respond. If their window is narrow, those requirements exceed their capacity. The words cannot get in.

So what does repair look like when words are not the way in?

Think of it less as repairing something that broke and more as re-establishing a pair. Two devices that lost their connection. Like Bluetooth. You do not force the devices together. You do not hold them against each other and press buttons until they sync. You bring them into range. You make sure both are discoverable. You wait for the connection to re-establish on its own.

You cannot rush the pairing. But you can make sure you are available for it.

This is (Re)Pair. Not fixing the moment. Reconnecting the pair.

The (Re)Pair spectrum

The right repair is the one your child's window can hold right now. Not the one that makes you feel most resolved. Not the one that seems most complete. The one that matches their current capacity.

At the most basic level, when the window is closed or nearly closed, (Re)Pair is ambient. No words. No demands. You walk into the room and sit down. You put food nearby. You exist in their space without requiring anything. No mention of what happened. No eye contact required. No acknowledgment expected. You are broadcasting one signal: I am here. There is no demand attached to my being here.

This looks like: placing a bowl of crackers outside their door and saying nothing. Sitting on the other end of the couch while they are on their device, not speaking, not looking at them, just present. Turning on their favorite show in the living room and happening to be there. Existing in the shared space without making the shared space about anything.

A step up, when the window is beginning to open but is still narrow, (Re)Pair is physical. Proximity and warmth, without language about the rupture. A hand on a shoulder if they tolerate touch. Sitting next to them, slightly closer than ambient but still not requiring engagement. Offering a blanket. Being the person who is near when they are ready for near.

This looks like: sitting on the end of their bed in silence. After a few minutes, they lean slightly toward you. That lean is data. The system is opening. You do not escalate. You do not start talking. You receive the lean. You stay.

A step further, when the window is partially open, (Re)Pair is named. A short, clean acknowledgment. One sentence. No justification. No explanation. No expectation of response. "I came in too hard this morning. That was too much pressure." Then nothing. The sentence is the repair. What follows the sentence is silence, not a follow-up question, not a processing conversation, not "do you want to talk about it."

And at the widest window, when the child is clearly regulated, when they have initiated conversation or eye contact, when the relationship feels settled enough to hold it, (Re)Pair can be conversational. A brief exchange about what happened. Not a post-mortem. Not a thirty-minute processing session. A short conversation driven by genuine curiosity. "Can I ask what that felt like from where you were?" And then actually listening. Not to defend yourself. Not to explain. To understand.

Most repair in PDA families happens in the first two categories: ambient and physical. That is not lesser repair. It is sometimes the only repair that actually lands. A parent who sits outside their child's door in silence for twenty minutes after a rupture, not speaking, not knocking, just available, is doing repair work that is more powerful than any apology, because it communicates something the nervous system trusts more than words: this person is still here and they are not requiring anything from me.

The way back in is often not a conversation

After a rupture, the path back to connection often does not look like talking about what happened. It looks like play. Silliness. An inside joke. A game started without asking if they want to play. A funny voice. A shared reference that belongs only to the two of you. A meme sent from the next room. An offer of food made with a slight smile and no gravity.

This is repair through the relationship itself. Rebuilding the connection through shared experience rather than processing the break. For many demand sensitive children, this is the only form of repair that does not carry demand. Processing is a demand. Talking about feelings is a demand. Explaining what happened is a demand. Playing is not. Laughing is not. Shared rhythm is not.

If the first thing that happens after a rupture is your child making a joke, or starting to narrate their game out loud, or sitting one cushion closer: that is their repair. That is them coming back into range. That is the Bluetooth reconnecting. Do not name it. Do not say "I'm glad you're feeling better." Do not use it as an opening to discuss what happened. Receive it the way you would receive any connection bid: quietly, without intensity, matching their energy. The repair is happening. Let it happen.

What parents long for

There is something underneath all of this that is worth naming.

You want to connect with your child. You want to play games with them. Be silly with them. Laugh with them. You want the easy moments that other families seem to have without trying. And the hardest part of parenting a demand sensitive child is that those moments can feel impossibly rare, because so much of your energy goes into crisis and recovery.

(Re)Pair is how those moments come back. Not as a reward for doing the framework correctly. Not on a schedule you can predict. But when you consistently show up as a safe, available presence, when you make bids for connection without attaching demands to them, when you repair without requiring anything in return, your child's nervous system starts to accumulate evidence that being in relationship with you is not a threat.

And when that evidence reaches a tipping point, the play comes. The silliness comes. The inside joke arrives. Not because you engineered it. Because the conditions finally allowed it.

(Re)Pair builds toward something larger than recovery from the last rupture. It builds toward a relationship your child's nervous system can rest in. That relationship is the infrastructure the entire framework depends on. Every pillar, every ADAPT cycle, every play in the playbook works better inside a relationship that has been repaired consistently over time.

You will get it wrong. You will repair. You will get it wrong again. You will repair again. The cycle is not a sign of failure. It is the mechanism. The relationship is not built by getting it right. It is built by coming back after getting it wrong.

That is the work. And you are already doing it.

PART FIVE

The Long Game

PART FIVE

Chapter 16: Talking to Your Child's Team

Your child does not exist inside your house alone. They exist inside a system: school, therapy, extended family, medical appointments, community activities, and every other setting where someone has expectations of them. Each of those settings has its own demand load. Each of those people has their own understanding, or misunderstanding, of what your child needs.

You have the framework now. You know what demand sensitivity is. You know the mechanisms. You know what works and what makes things worse. The problem is that most of the people in your child's life do not know any of this, and some of them are actively doing the things that make it worse, with good intentions and no awareness of the damage.

This chapter is about bringing the people around your child into the picture. Not by converting them to the RELATE framework. Not by requiring them to read this book. By giving them enough information, in the right format, to change what your child's nervous system encounters when it encounters them.

The one-sentence opener

Most conversations about your child's needs will go better if you start with one sentence:

"My child's nervous system processes demands as threats."

That sentence does more work than a diagnosis code. It is specific enough to be meaningful. It is accessible enough to be understood by someone who has never heard of PDA. It immediately reframes the conversation away from behavior (they are defiant, they are oppositional, they are manipulative, they are lazy) and toward mechanism (their nervous system is doing something that produces these behaviors).

You do not need to explain PDA. You do not need to provide a research summary. You do not need to name the three mechanisms or describe the framework. You need one sentence that lands in the other person's understanding and shifts what they think they are looking at. That sentence is it.

What follows the sentence depends on who you are talking to and what you need from them.

When school will not accommodate

Most teachers are not difficult people. They are people operating inside a system that was designed for neurotypical nervous systems, with class sizes that do not allow for individualized response, under pressure to meet benchmarks that assume a baseline of compliance. When your child does not meet that baseline, the teacher reaches for the tools they have: consequences, redirection, behavioral plans, calls home. Those tools work for most students. For your child, they add demand to an overloaded system.

Start small. Specific. One accommodation at a time.

"Can my child have five minutes of transition time between activities?" is more likely to succeed than "my child needs a completely different approach." The first request is concrete, bounded, and easy to implement. The second is overwhelming and vague. Build from the first. Once the teacher sees that five minutes of transition time reduces meltdowns by half, the conversation about the next accommodation is easier.

Bring data. The demand audit is powerful in school meetings because it makes visible something that school professionals have never counted. The number of demands in a school day (transitions, instructions, social expectations, compliance requirements, sensory inputs, schedule changes) is almost always shocking to someone who has never added them up. When you show a teacher that your child encounters sixty to eighty demands in a school day, and that their nervous system processes each one through a threat-detection system, the teacher begins to understand why the afternoon collapse happens. They begin to see the school day as a cumulative load rather than a series of individual choices your child is making badly.

Bring the One-Page Summary. The full worksheet is in the Appendix (Tool 8). Fill it out and bring it to every meeting about your child. It gives the school exactly what they need on a single sheet: what helps your child feel safe, what makes things harder, current intense interests (regulation tools, not rewards), biggest demand triggers, what escalation looks like, what shutdown looks like, what to do when it happens, what not to do, best way to communicate with your child, and your contact information. One page. Hand it over and say: "This is what works and what does not work for my child. Can we start here?"

When the school pushes back, document everything. Request formal meetings and put everything in writing. Many schools respond to specific, documented requests more readily than to verbal conversations. "Per our meeting on [date], we agreed to [specific accommodation]. I want to confirm this is in place." Paper trails matter. Not because you are building a legal case. Because institutional systems respond to documentation in ways they do not respond to conversation.

Lead with the mechanism, not the label. "My child's nervous system processes demands as threats" opens more doors than "my child has PDA" because PDA is not widely known in school systems and the word "pathological" creates resistance before the conversation starts. The mechanism is what the school needs to understand. The label is secondary.

If the school is actively harmful (using coercive methods, punishing demand avoidance, isolating your child, restraining without justification) you may need to escalate beyond the classroom teacher. Request meetings with administration. Bring documentation. Know your rights under your country's or state's disability and education laws. This book cannot provide legal advice, but organizations like the PDA Society and PDA North America maintain resources on educational advocacy.

When your child's therapist does not understand PDA

This happens more often than it should. Many therapists who work with children use compliance-based models: behavioral activation, CBT frameworks that treat avoidance as a target to be overcome, exposure hierarchies that assume gradual tolerance-building works for all anxiety presentations, motivational interviewing techniques that assume a level of demand tolerance that PDA individuals may not have.

If your child is in therapy and consistently worse after sessions, that is data. If the therapist frames your child's avoidance as a choice, that is data. If they push compliance as the goal, use behavioral contracts, or tell you that your child needs firmer limits, that is data.

That data does not necessarily mean the therapist is bad at their job. It may mean they are applying a model that works for most anxious children and does not work for yours. The distinction matters because a therapist who is skilled but working from the wrong model can often adjust if given the right information. A therapist who is unskilled is a different problem.

What to try first: share information. "I want to share something about my child's profile that I think is relevant to the work you're doing." Hand them this book, or point them to the clinical manual (the RELATE Foundational Training Manual at relatepda.com). A good therapist will read it, or at least engage with the framework, and adjust their approach. A therapist who dismisses the information or insists that their current model is sufficient despite evidence of worsening is a therapist whose model is more important to them than your child's nervous system. That is your signal to find someone else.

When looking for a new therapist, ask directly: how do you work with children who have strong autonomy needs and who respond to demands with avoidance? What does your approach look like when a client refuses to engage with a therapeutic task? Have you worked with pathological demand avoidance specifically? The answers will tell you what you need to know. You are listening for: flexibility, willingness to follow the child's lead, comfort with non-compliance, and absence of coercive language.

Red flags in treatment: behavioral contracts with consequences. Graduated exposure hierarchies applied without assessing the window. Group therapy programs that use peer pressure or confrontation. Any program that frames demand avoidance as a choice to be motivated away. Residential treatment and wilderness therapy programs warrant particular caution. Many use coercive models that are poorly suited to PDA profiles and have produced significant harm in neurodivergent young people.

When your child will not engage with any provider

For some families, the barrier is not finding the right provider. It is that their child has reached a point where they refuse all professional contact. They will not go to a therapist. They will not get in the car. They will not engage with an evaluator. They have learned, through experience, that "help" is another source of demands they cannot meet.

If this is your situation, you are not out of options. The work may need to start with you and the professionals working together without your child in the room. You adjust the environment. You reduce the demand load. You build the conditions under which your child's nervous system might eventually tolerate support. A therapist working with you on strategy, coaching you through the framework, helping you work through specific situations: that counts as seeking help. It just does not look like what most people picture.

If your child is in crisis (expressing suicidal thoughts, engaging in self-harm, not eating, not leaving their room for days, physically aggressive in ways that create safety risk) a book is not enough. Please seek professional help. Call 988 (Suicide and Crisis Lifeline), text HOME to 741741 (Crisis Text Line), or go to your nearest emergency room. ADAPT from Chapter 9 applies for in-the-moment support while you seek professional help. Safety comes first. This book will be here when the immediate crisis has passed.

Talking to your child about what they already feel

Your child likely already knows something is different about them. They have watched themselves refuse things they wanted to do. They have felt the panic when a simple request landed like an attack. They have seen their peers handle things that feel impossible to them. They may not have words for it, but they have the experience.

The question is not whether to tell them. It is whether to give them language for what they already feel.

This is not a diagnostic disclosure. It is not sitting them down for a clinical conversation. It is giving your child words.

Something like: "Your brain works differently with expectations. That is why some things feel impossible even when you want to do them. It is not your fault."

That is all they may need to hear for now. You are not labeling them. You are naming what they already live with. If they want to know more, offer more. If they change the subject, let them. The conversation is available when they are ready for it.

Timing matters. Do not have this conversation during a crisis, after a meltdown, or when tensions are high. Wait for a moment when the window is wide, when they are curious, calm, or asking questions about why things are hard for them. If the conversation emerges from their curiosity, it lands better than if it arrives as your agenda.

What not to do. Do not use PDA or demand sensitivity as an excuse: "you can't help it, so it's fine." That removes agency and communicates that nothing is expected of them. Do not make it sound like something is wrong with them. Do not frame it as a limitation. Frame it as a difference: their nervous system has a protective system that is more sensitive than most. There is nothing wrong with that. It needs understanding, not correction.

Some children are not ready for this conversation. If your child is very young, or in a period of high distress, the words can wait. What cannot wait is the shift in how you respond to them. They will feel the difference in your approach long before they have language for why.

How to know it is working

You will not see dramatic improvement. You will see quiet shifts that accumulate.

Recovery time after meltdowns is getting shorter. Meltdown intensity is decreasing, even if the frequency has not changed yet. Your child is initiating contact or conversation more often. The repair cycle is tightening. You catch your patterns sooner and repair faster. Your child is tolerating small demands they previously could not. Your own nervous system is more stable. You are spending less time outside your window. You are catching your demand-placing patterns before they escalate instead of after.

None of these are dramatic. All of them are real. They are the metrics that matter, and they are the metrics that most people around you will not notice, because they are looking for the old metrics: compliance, attendance, performance. The old metrics measure whether the behavior changed. The new metrics measure whether the nervous system is building capacity. Those are different questions with different timelines and different answers.

If you are not seeing any movement after three months of consistent implementation, seek professional consultation. That is not failure. That is accurate assessment of a situation that may need additional support.

RELATE consultations are available at relatepda.com. The framework is the tool. Professional guidance is how you troubleshoot the tool when the situation is more complex than a book can address.

PART FIVE

Chapter 17: Your Partner, Your Family, Your Identity

The framework operates inside your home. But your home is not isolated. It sits inside a network of relationships that have their own expectations, their own understandings, and their own demands on you. Your partner or co-parent, who may or may not be on the same page. Your other children, who are watching everything. Your extended family, who have opinions. And you, the person underneath the PDA parent, who may have forgotten what you look like apart from this role.

This chapter addresses all four. None of them have clean resolutions. What this chapter offers is honest framing and, where possible, practical structure.

Co-parent disagreement

If your partner or co-parent does not yet understand demand sensitivity, this may be the hardest part of your situation.

You are implementing RELATE while someone in the same household is implementing consequences. You are lowering demands while they are holding the line. You are reading the window while they are reading the behavior. That inconsistency is not just frustrating for you. It is genuinely confusing for your child's nervous system, which encounters two radically different environments depending on which parent is in the room.

The most common forms of misalignment: one parent has understood the PDA framework and changed their approach significantly. The other has not, or has partially. One parent is setting limits (ultimatums, financial pressure, deadlines) and the other is absorbing the consequences of those limits. One parent blames the other's "enabling" for the situation. The other blames the first parent's "pressure" for the escalations.

Both parents are usually right about something. Both parents are usually wrong about something. And your child is living inside the contradiction, which is its own demand load.

You cannot force your partner to change. That sentence is hard to read if you are the parent who understands the framework and watches the other parent do the things you know will make it worse. But forcing your partner to adopt RELATE is itself a demand on them, and if their nervous system responds to that demand with resistance, you are now in a compliance loop with your co-parent that mirrors the compliance loop Chapter 14 described with your child. The mechanism is the same. Pressure produces resistance. More pressure produces more resistance.

What works instead: lead with outcomes, not theory. "Here is what I've been trying. Here is what has changed." That is a more compelling conversation than "here is the framework I want you to adopt." Concrete, observable results. "I stopped saying 'get dressed' and started putting clothes on the chair without a word. The morning took fifteen minutes instead of forty-five." "I stopped repeating myself and the meltdown was shorter." Your partner does not need to understand the neuroscience. They need to see that something different is working.

Share Chapter 1 of this book. It is the shortest, most accessible explanation of what is happening in your child's nervous system. If your partner will read one chapter, that is the one. If they will not read anything, do not push it. Pushing it is a demand. Instead, keep doing what works and let the results speak.

Find the minimum viable overlap. You do not need full alignment. You need one shared agreement. What is the one approach you are both willing to commit to consistently for the next month? "We will both use declarative language instead of direct commands." "We will both drop demands when we see the window closing." "Neither of us will use consequences as a response to avoidance." One thing. Not the whole framework. One thing.

That one commitment, held consistently by both parents, shifts the household demand load more than you might expect. It gives your child's nervous system one consistent signal from both adults instead of contradictory signals. Build from there. One agreement that works becomes the foundation for the second agreement. The second becomes the foundation for the third. Alignment built incrementally through shared experience is stronger than alignment demanded all at once through theory.

If the divide is deep, consider working with a therapist who understands neurodivergence. Not to fix your partner. Not to prove you are right. To build a shared understanding of what your child's nervous system needs, mediated by someone who is not invested in being right about the approach. A good family therapist can hold both perspectives and help you find the overlap that matters.

If your partner will not engage with any of this, at any level, that is painful and it is real. A child with one consistently regulated, low-demand parent has a significantly different experience than a child with none. Your work matters even when it is not matched. Your child's nervous system knows which parent is safe. That knowledge is a deposit in the account, even when the other parent is making withdrawals.

Siblings

The sibling dynamic is one of the most painful parts of this experience. You are not doing something wrong. The math just does not work.

One child's nervous system requires enormous accommodation. There are only so many hours and so much capacity in a day. The other children notice. They notice the different rules, the different expectations, the different amount of attention. They notice that the crisis always belongs to one child and the rest of them work around it.

Siblings may feel invisible. They may feel confused about why the rules are different. They may feel scared by the meltdowns. They may feel angry that they are expected to be flexible, patient, and understanding while their sibling appears to get away with everything. All of those responses make sense. Every one of them is valid.

You do not need to fix this perfectly. You need to name it honestly and respond to it consistently.

Age-appropriate language helps. For younger siblings: "Your sibling's brain works differently with expectations. That is why things look different for them sometimes. That does not mean your feelings matter less." For older siblings who can handle more complexity: "Your sibling has a nervous system that experiences everyday demands as threats. The accommodations we make are not about fairness. They are about giving each of you what you need. What you need matters too, and I want to hear what that is."

Give siblings permission to feel frustrated, jealous, sad, and angry about the situation without making them feel guilty for having those feelings. "It's okay to be mad about this" is more useful than "try to understand." Understanding may come later. Permission to feel what they feel comes first.

Protect one-on-one time with each child. Even fifteen minutes where your non-PDA child has your undivided, uninterrupted attention. It does not have to be elaborate. It does not have to be an outing or a special activity. It has to be theirs. Not rescheduled because their sibling had a crisis. Not interrupted by a text about what is happening at home. Not spent talking about the PDA sibling's needs.

That last part is the hardest and it is the most important. If one-on-one time with your non-PDA child is consistently sacrificed for the PDA child's crises, the sibling's experience of invisibility is being confirmed every time. They learn: when it matters, I come second. That learning compounds the same way relational deposits compound, except in the wrong direction.

If the sibling dynamic is creating persistent distress (one child consistently withdrawing, acting out, expressing a stuck sense of unfairness that is not resolving, developing their own anxiety or behavioral changes in response to the household stress) family therapy with a provider who understands both PDA and family systems can help. This is not a sign that you have failed to balance things. It is a sign that the situation is genuinely difficult and the whole family could use support.

Your identity beyond PDA parent

It is not dramatic to say that parenting a demand sensitive child is a consuming identity. For many parents in this situation, the crisis has lasted long enough and with enough intensity that other aspects of who you are have gradually receded.

The career that used to matter. The friendships that required a reciprocity you no longer had the capacity for. The interests that needed time and attention the crisis absorbed. The marriage or partnership that needed presence you were spending elsewhere. The person you were before this became the central fact of your daily life.

This is not a character failure. It is what happens when a high-demand, invisible crisis occupies your life for years without adequate support. It is a predictable outcome of the situation, not evidence that you have lost yourself.

Naming it matters because rebuilding something outside the crisis is not optional. It is not a luxury you earn after things stabilize. It is part of the framework.

Here is why: a parent whose entire identity is organized around managing their PDA child's life is more likely to transmit the invisible demands of that investment to their child's nervous system. Your child's system reads your state constantly. A parent whose internal world is entirely organized around the child's needs broadcasts that organization as a frequency the child can feel. It registers as: I am the center of this person's existence. My needs are the thing this person's life is about. That sounds like it should feel good. For a demand sensitive nervous system, it is its own kind of pressure. The weight of being the thing your parent's entire life is organized around is a demand. A large one.

A parent who is, gradually, finding their way back to something outside the crisis is better co-regulation infrastructure than a parent whose entire nervous system is organized around the child's. Not because the outside thing matters more than the child. Because the outside thing gives your nervous system somewhere to exist that is not the crisis. That existence, that small pocket of identity that is not about PDA, reduces what you transmit. It settles the frequency. Your child encounters a parent who has a life, not just a role. That is more regulating than it sounds.

What rebuilding looks like: not a dramatic pivot. Not a vacation that solves everything. Small and consistent reallocation of something to yourself. One hour a week that is non-negotiably yours. Not for errands. Not for PDA research. Yours. One relationship outside the PDA world that does not require you to translate your life before you can be in it. One thing you are interested in that has nothing to do with your child's nervous system. A walk. A book that is not about parenting. A class. A conversation with a friend about something other than what happened this week.

These are not luxuries. They are what sustains the capacity to continue.

A note on parent PDA

Many parents of demand sensitive children have demand sensitivity themselves. Often identified through their child's process. You read the descriptions of PDA in Part 1 and something landed differently. Not just recognition of your child. Recognition of yourself.

If that is you, the dynamics described in this book run in both directions. Your child's demand avoidance activates your own. Your own demand avoidance affects your capacity to sustain the low-demand presence the framework asks for. The co-parent disagreement may be complicated by your nervous system's response to the demands of the disagreement itself. The demand audit on your own life may reveal that your system is processing demands the same way your child's does, just with different strategies and more practice at masking.

This is not a problem to fix before you can use the framework. It is context that matters. Knowing you have demand sensitivity yourself changes what you expect of yourself, how you design your own demand reduction, and how you understand the moments when you cannot sustain what the framework asks of you. Those moments are not failure. They are your nervous system doing the same thing your child's nervous system does. The same compassion you are learning to extend to your child applies to you.

The adult book, currently in development, is written for exactly this situation. If you recognized yourself while reading about your child, that recognition is real, and there will be a guide that speaks to it directly. In the meantime, the framework in this book applies to you in the same way it applies to your child: change the conditions the nervous system encounters, and the nervous system responds differently.

PART FIVE

Chapter 18: The Autonomy Shift

Everything in Parts 1 through 4 was written to be age-neutral. The six pillars do not change because your child turned fourteen. ADAPT does not expire at eighteen. The demand audit is as relevant at seventeen as it is at seven. The mechanisms (subcortical threat detection, Intolerance of Uncertainty, perceived loss of autonomy) do not upgrade themselves out of a person as they grow older.

But the application changes. Significantly.

If your child is a teenager or young adult, this chapter and the next are for you. If your child is younger, you can read these now for the long view or come back to them later. The framework is the same. The territory is different.

Why everything shifts

Three things change during adolescence and young adulthood that make this chapter necessary rather than optional.

The first: autonomy is no longer yours to grant.

With a young child, you are the environmental architect. You control the schedule, the food, the social calendar, the sensory environment. You grant autonomy in measured doses. Choices within a framework you designed. That arrangement works, more or less, because your child is small and the world is mostly you.

By adolescence, that arrangement is over. Autonomy is being claimed whether you grant it or not. Your teenager's nervous system is driving them toward independence at exactly the same time their demand sensitive profile makes the demands of independence feel intolerable. The push toward autonomy and the terror of its requirements are happening simultaneously, inside the same person. And they are taking it out on the nearest available target, which is you.

By young adulthood, autonomy is not just claimed. It is legally theirs. You cannot force a nineteen-year-old to shower, apply for a job, see a therapist, or leave their room. You can encourage. You can support. You can accommodate. You can grieve. You cannot compel. The sooner you make peace with that reality, the more useful you become to them.

The second: the demands changed.

Morning routines and homework were the daily battlefield when your child was nine. Those battles were exhausting and real. But the stakes were bounded. A missed school day. A skipped shower. An unfinished assignment. The stakes are different now. School dropout. Employment, or the absence of it. Leaving the house. Substance use. Relationships, and the demand dynamics inside them. Hygiene that has crossed into health concern. Medical avoidance. Whether they will ever be able to live independently.

The demands also shifted location. When your child was young, the demands were primarily domestic. You could see them. You could audit them. Now they come from everywhere. The social world. The job market. The legal and financial systems. Their own internal pressure to be further along than they are. You have less visibility and less control over most of what is activating their threat response, and more is at stake.

The third: the relationship has history.

If your child is fifteen, you have fifteen years between you. If they are twenty-two, you have twenty-two years. Some of that history is good. Repair that landed. Connection that accumulated. Moments your child's nervous system filed away as evidence that this relationship was safe.

But for most families reading this chapter, a significant portion of that history is something else. It is the reward chart that never worked, applied for two years anyway. It is the school that insisted on compliance and you trusted them. It is the therapist who said your child needed "firmer limits" and you followed that advice because you did not know better. It is every consequence, every "you're capable of this when you try," every morning you lost your temper before 8 AM for six years because no one told you what was actually happening.

Your child's nervous system recorded all of it. The fact that you did not know does not erase what their system registered. The repair work is different when there are years of relational debt. Not days. Years. That is the reality this chapter addresses.

The control paradox

The clinical pattern is consistent enough to state plainly: the more you try to control a PDA teenager, the less functional the relationship becomes and the less your teenager moves toward capacity. The less you try to control, the more space their nervous system has to move toward you and, occasionally, toward function.

This feels, to almost every parent in this situation, like giving up. It is not giving up.

Giving up looks like disconnecting. Checking out. Stopping caring. Letting the relationship dissolve into a household of cohabitating strangers who share a kitchen and nothing else.

Releasing control looks like: "I'm not going to push you on this today. I'm here if you want to talk about it." And meaning it. And still being there tomorrow. And the day after. Without commentary on what they did or did not do in the meantime.

The line between them is not the words. It is the tone, the presence, and the follow-through over months. Your teenager's nervous system can tell the difference between a parent who has given up and a parent who has released control. Given up feels like absence. Released control feels like presence without pressure. The first is abandonment. The second is the hardest form of parenting available.

Releasing control requires you to hold your anxiety about their future without transmitting it to them as pressure. It requires watching them make choices you would not make and staying present without commentary. It requires tolerating the gap between where they are and where you think they should be without letting that gap become a demand they can feel in every interaction.

Your visible worry is a demand. Your unspoken comparison to their peers is a demand. Your disappointment when they do not follow through is a demand. The face you make when you see them gaming at 2 PM on a Tuesday is a demand. None of these are demands you intend to place. All of them register in a nervous system that has been reading your state for their entire life.

Autonomy does not mean abandonment

One of the most common traps parents fall into when they first understand the control paradox is swinging to a false opposite. If pushing does not work, maybe I should disengage. If presence feels like pressure, maybe I should be less present.

That is not the model.

"I'm not going to force you" is different from "I don't care what you do." The first preserves the relationship while respecting their nervous system. The second communicates disconnection. A PDA teenager's system is exquisitely sensitive to that difference.

You can lower demands, eliminate forced compliance, stop the battles over hygiene and bedtime and screen time, and still be a warm, present, available parent. You can stop pushing the job conversation and still sit near them while they play games. You can release every explicit demand and still be the person whose presence communicates: I am here. I am not going anywhere. I am not measuring you.

Presence without agenda is one of the most powerful things you can offer a PDA teenager. It is almost never what they had before.

What the shift looks like at different ages

At thirteen to fifteen, the shift is often sudden and confusing. The approach that worked at eleven stops working at fourteen. Your child is pushing back on every explicit demand but still needs you significantly more than they can admit. What helps: back off explicit demands while maintaining a thick presence of availability. This is the age where reducing direct requests while increasing low-demand connection time produces the most traction. Be Near. Follow In. Offer Without Requiring. The emotional and relational demands you place invisibly (your worry, your disappointment, your timeline for them) become the demands that matter most. The explicit demands are easier to identify and lower. The invisible ones are harder.

At sixteen to eighteen, most PDA teenagers are in some kind of standoff with the world. School may be in crisis or already over. The outside world is placing real demands: grades, driving tests, college applications, part-time jobs. Most of those demands are beyond the current window. What helps: moving fully into the consultant role. Your job is not to manage their schedule or enforce attendance. It is to be available when they want input, to offer genuine choices without attaching outcomes, and to reduce the ambient demand load of the household as much as possible. When they ask for your opinion, give it once. Do not repeat it. Do not check whether they followed it. The opinion was offered. What they do with it is theirs.

At nineteen to twenty-five, the gap between legal status and nervous system capacity becomes most visible and most painful. Your child is legally an adult. Their nervous system may still be operating at the regulatory capacity of a much younger person, particularly if the demand load has been chronically overwhelming for years. What helps: stopping. Stopping the expectation that "launching" looks like what it looks like for neurotypical young adults. Stopping the timeline comparison. The twenty-one-year-old still in their room needs you to stop solving and start witnessing. They need you to communicate, through your behavior over months, that you are not going anywhere and you are not measuring them against a benchmark they cannot meet.

Connection when the door is closed

Chapter 7 teaches five modes of low-demand connection. With teenagers, particularly those who have retreated to their room and closed the door, those modes need adaptation.

Be Near looks different when the door is closed. You cannot be in the same room if they have made the room inaccessible. Be Near becomes: being in the house. Being audibly present (moving in the kitchen, making food, existing in the shared spaces) without approaching the door. The signal is not "I am watching you." It is "I am here, living my life, and the space is available if you want it."

Follow In may happen entirely through a screen. If your teenager is gaming and will not tolerate your physical presence, watching a stream of their game (if they stream) or asking a single question about the game via text is Follow In adapted for a closed door. If they share a meme or a video with you, that is a connection bid. Respond to it. Match their energy. Do not escalate it into a conversation about how they are doing.

Offer Without Requiring adapts well to a closed door. Food left outside the door. A drink placed without a knock. A text that says "there's pizza on the counter" with no follow-up. A link to something related to their interest sent with no expectation of response. These offers cross the barrier of the closed door without demanding that it open.

Shared Rhythm is the hardest to maintain when connection is minimal. Car rides remain one of the best options, if your teenager will get in the car. A drive with no destination and their music playing is Shared Rhythm. If they will not leave the house, parallel screen time (both of you gaming in adjacent spaces, or you watching something in the living room while they are in their room) is a distant version of Shared Rhythm. It is not nothing. It is two nervous systems in the same house doing parallel activities. That is a thread of connection, even when it does not feel like one.

The scenarios that keep you awake

Several situations specific to the teen and young adult years deserve direct attention. Not in the full scenario format of Chapter 10, but as honest discussions of what these situations look like and what the framework offers.

The teenager who will not leave their room. They are in there. The door is closed. They come out for food, sometimes. They are on screens all day and most of the night. Their sleep schedule is inverted. You do not know what they are doing in there and the not-knowing is its own kind of torment. What RELATE suggests: the room is their retreat space. It is the lowest-demand environment available to them. They are not hiding. They are surviving. Reduce demands on the rest of the household so the space outside the room becomes lower-demand too. Offer without requiring. Be present in the house. Do not set timers on how long they can be in their room. Do not threaten to remove the door. Do not cut the wifi as leverage. Each of those actions removes the one safe space they have and teaches their nervous system that even safety is contingent on compliance.

School dropout. Your teenager has stopped attending school. The calls from the school have stopped because the school has given up or you have formally withdrawn them. You are terrified about what this means for their future. What RELATE suggests: school dropout in PDA is a capacity problem, not a motivation problem. The cumulative demand load of school exceeded the window and the system crashed. Forcing return during the crash extends the recovery. What the nervous system needs is demand reduction (at home, not just school), time, and a gradual reintroduction of structure at the edges of the window. That may mean partial attendance later. It may mean alternative education. It may mean a long period of nothing that looks productive while the nervous system recovers. The timeline is not yours to set. Your anxiety about the timeline is understandable. Transmitting that anxiety to your teenager as pressure makes the recovery longer, not shorter.

Substance use. Some PDA teenagers use substances to manage the demand load. Alcohol, cannabis, and other substances reduce threat activation, lower inhibition, and create a temporary window of tolerance that the nervous system cannot produce on its own. This is self-medication, not recreation. It makes neurological sense even as it creates additional problems. What RELATE suggests: address it as a demand-management strategy, not a behavioral problem. The question is not "how do I stop them from using." The question is "what demand load is this substance managing, and can I help reduce that load through other means?" This does not mean you ignore dangerous use. If substance use has created a medical emergency or is putting them or others at direct risk, that is a crisis situation requiring professional intervention, not a parenting framework. But short of crisis, the demand-reduction approach is more likely to reduce use over time than consequences, confrontation, or coerced treatment. Removing the substance without addressing the demand load it was managing leaves the load unmanaged. Something else will fill the gap, and it may be worse.

Relationships. Your teenager's relationships are complicated by their demand sensitivity in ways that are hard to name without pathologizing them. They may connect intensely and then disappear completely. They may form close bonds online with people they have never met and resist all in-person connection. They may be in a relationship that concerns you. What RELATE suggests: the demand dynamics of PDA operate inside relationships the same way they operate outside them. The social withdrawal pattern (intense connection followed by disappearance) is the demand load of sustained relationship exceeding the window. Close relationships carry demands: being available, being consistent, responding to messages, showing up. When the window narrows, those demands become intolerable and disappearance is the most accessible response. You cannot manage your teenager's relationships. You can maintain a relationship with them that is safe enough for them to bring concerns to you when they have them. "I'm interested in who matters to you. You don't have to tell me everything, but I'm here when you want to." Then hold the door open. If a relationship concerns you because it appears harmful, say something once, clearly, without pressure for a response. Then do not bring it up again unless they do. Repeated commentary on a harmful relationship closes the door to that conversation rather than opening it.

The young adult who will not launch. They are nineteen, twenty-one, twenty-three. Still at home. No job. No school. No visible trajectory. You are fielding questions from family. You are watching your financial situation adjust to accommodate someone who, by conventional measures, should be independent. What RELATE suggests: begin by being honest with yourself about what "launching" means versus what it might mean for your specific young adult. Conventional launching (out of the house by twenty-two, employed, increasingly independent) may not be accessible on that timeline, or ever in exactly that form. What launching looks like for a PDA nervous system is nonlinear, slower, and often does not follow the expected sequence. The apartment may come before the job. Both may come years later than expected, after a period of apparent stagnation that was actually nervous system recovery the outside world cannot see. The pressure to launch, even unspoken, is a demand. It activates threat. Have the conversation that explicitly separates your relationship from their productivity. "I love you the same regardless of whether this happens this year or five years from now." Say it once. Mean it. Then behave in accordance with it consistently over months.

Sustaining this

Part 4 of this book (Chapters 12 through 15) applies to parents of teenagers and young adults with more urgency than it does to parents of younger children. You have been doing this longer. You have had less success and less rest. Your burnout is likely deeper. Your patterns are more deeply wired. Your grief is older and heavier.

Sustaining the work at this stage requires, at minimum: other people who understand what you are living with. Other parents in similar situations. A therapist who does not require you to perform perspective or progress. People who can hold the weight without trying to fix it or redirect you to gratitude.

Your own regulation practices, maintained even when time and energy are scarce. Because a depleted parent supporting a PDA young adult produces two depleted nervous systems in the same house. The co-regulation mechanism does not stop operating because your child turned eighteen. If anything, it matters more now, because you have fewer tools available (you cannot control the environment the way you could when they were seven) and the relationship is the primary tool that remains.

And permission, from yourself, from this book, from whoever you need it from, to not be okay. To be struggling with this. To not have made your peace with it yet. To be angry and scared and exhausted. The work requires your presence, not your performed resolution. You do not need to have accepted this situation in order to be useful inside it. You need to show up, as regulated as you can manage, as often as you can manage, for as long as it takes.

PART FIVE

Chapter 19: The Questions That Keep You Up at Night

This chapter addresses the fears you think about at 2 AM. The ones you type into search engines and then delete. The ones you are afraid to say out loud because saying them makes them more real, and you are not sure you can handle them being more real than they already are.

Some of these questions have answers that are actually reassuring. Some of them have honest answers that are not. You have been given false reassurance before. Parents in your situation always have. "It will get better." "They'll grow out of it." "Just be consistent." None of that helped, and some of it delayed the real work by years. What you will find here is honesty. That is harder than reassurance, but it is more useful.

"Will they ever be independent?"

The honest answer: maybe. But independence may not look like what you pictured, and the timeline is not yours to set.

Independence for a demand sensitive nervous system is slower than the conventional sequence. It is more nonlinear. It often does not follow the expected order of education, then employment, then housing, then relationships, unfolding neatly between eighteen and twenty-five. Some steps may happen out of sequence. Some may happen much later. Some may happen in forms that do not match the benchmark.

For some PDA young adults, a version of conventional independence becomes accessible over time. Not at twenty-two, but at twenty-six or thirty or differently at every age. Part-time work in a self-directed environment. Shared housing with someone whose demand style is compatible. Independent management of basic life tasks in a space they have designed for their own nervous system. That is real independence. It does not need to match the picture in order to count.

For others, supported independence is the realistic long-term trajectory. Housing with some support infrastructure. Work that is structured around their specific capacity. Financial support that does not come with demands attached. That is also a real and valuable life. It is a life with dignity and agency and connection and meaning. It is not the life you imagined, and the grief of that gap is real (Chapter 6 named it and it applies here with full force), but it is a life worth building toward and a life worth living.

What the framework is building toward is nervous system capacity: the ability to tolerate more demand, more uncertainty, more of the requirements of adult life, over time, gradually. The work is not building toward a specific outcome. It is building the capacity that makes outcomes possible. Which outcomes become accessible depends on the specific person, the specific nervous system, the support systems available, and how much demand reduction and relational safety were provided during the years when the foundation was being laid.

Your work right now is laying that foundation. You cannot control what gets built on it. You can make the foundation as solid as possible.

"Am I enabling them?"

This question keeps more parents awake than almost any other. It deserves a direct answer.

The word "enabling" comes from substance use treatment. It refers to removing consequences that a person needs to experience in order to change a harmful behavior. The underlying assumption is that consequences would produce change if the parent stopped shielding the person from them.

For PDA, that assumption is not accurate.

Consequences do not produce capacity in a demand sensitive nervous system. They produce activation. The nervous system does not evaluate the consequence, decide the cost is too high, and change the behavior. The nervous system encounters the consequence as a threat, activates, and either avoids harder or shuts down further. The consequence does not teach. It depletes.

Enabling and accommodating are different things.

Enabling removes consequences that would produce growth. Accommodating removes barriers the nervous system cannot currently overcome.

For most of what looks like "enabling" in PDA families (allowing your young adult to live at home, not pushing daily employment, accepting a lower standard of hygiene, not forcing treatment, letting them sleep until noon, not requiring them to do chores) the accurate word is accommodating. The barriers are real. Removing them does not prevent growth. It makes growth possible. A nervous system that is not in chronic activation has available capacity. Available capacity is what growth requires.

The test is not whether other people think you are enabling them. Extended family, friends, people who say "they just need a kick in the pants": their assessment is not the relevant data. They are not living inside your young adult's nervous system. They are not watching what the demand pressure produces.

The test is: is the current arrangement producing any movement toward capacity, however slow and nonlinear? Is your young adult's overall functioning stable, improving gradually, or declining?

If there is movement, even small and inconsistent (they showered twice this week when last month it was once, they mentioned something about maybe wanting a job even though they did not follow through, they came out of their room voluntarily more often, they are sleeping slightly less inverted, they tolerated a family dinner they would have refused six months ago) the accommodation is doing what it is supposed to do. It is creating the conditions in which the nervous system can build capacity at its own pace.

If there is no movement over months, or if functioning is actively declining, that is data that something additional is needed. Not consequences. Professional support. A clinical consultation to assess whether something else is going on (depression, trauma, substance use, medical issues) that is preventing the capacity-building the accommodation is designed to support.

"What happens when I'm gone?"

This is the long-term fear. It is one of the most legitimate. You are doing an enormous amount of invisible work to create the conditions in which your child can function. What happens when you are no longer here to do that work?

The honest answer is that the best time to address this question is now. Not when you are in crisis. Not when your health has changed. Not when the urgency becomes undeniable. Now, while you have capacity to think about it and act on it.

What planning looks like in practical terms:

Connecting with disability services in your area while your young adult is young enough to access them and before you are in crisis. Many services have waitlists. Getting on those waitlists now, even if the services are not needed yet, is a practical step that reduces the uncertainty of the future.

Establishing relationships with providers who understand PDA and who can maintain a relationship with your young adult over time. Not just your child's current therapist. A network of people who know your young adult, who understand the profile, and who can provide continuity of support that does not depend on you.

Investigating supported living options. Not because they are imminent. Because knowing what exists reduces the fear of the unknown. The fear is partly about the reality and partly about the blankness. Filling in the picture, even with options that are years away, gives the fear somewhere to land other than your chest at 2 AM.

Legal planning. Powers of attorney. Disability benefits. Supported decision-making documents. These can begin as soon as your young adult is of legal age. Beginning early, when the situation is stable, is significantly easier than beginning in crisis, when the situation is not.

Your other children are not the plan. If you have children who are less affected, the temptation to build your long-term plan around their sibling availability is understandable. Resist it. That arrangement places a burden on your other children that they did not choose and your PDA young adult did not consent to. The plan should be as independent of family expectation as you can make it, with family connection as a supplement rather than a foundation.

"Should I force the issue?"

You are thinking about an ultimatum. Get a job or move out. See a therapist or lose financial support. Go to the appointment or I will not pay for the medication. You are at the end of your rope and you believe that the current situation cannot continue.

Ultimatums are high-demand interventions. They produce compliance, crisis, or a combination of both. They rarely produce capacity.

Compliance produced by an ultimatum: your young adult gets a job because they have no alternative. They are holding that job from a depleted, activated nervous system, in an environment they did not choose, with consequences attached to staying. The demand load is enormous. The window narrows. The job ends, often quickly. The relationship has sustained additional damage because you used power to produce the compliance. The compliance was not capacity. It was performance under threat. And the performance could not sustain itself because the nervous system was not resourced to sustain it.

Crisis produced by an ultimatum: your young adult cannot comply. They know they cannot comply. The ultimatum becomes confirmation that the relationship is conditional on their performance. The rupture may be significant. It may take a long time to repair. It may produce outcomes (leaving the house without a plan, cutting off contact, escalation that involves authorities) that are worse than the situation the ultimatum was designed to address.

There are situations where intervention is necessary. When substance use has created a medical emergency. When your young adult's safety is at direct risk. When the situation in your home has become genuinely unsafe for other people in it. In those cases, intervention is appropriate. But the intervention should be clinical, not a parental ultimatum. Engaging a crisis team, a clinical intervention specialist, or a PDA-informed therapist to support the conversation produces better outcomes than unilateral pressure.

What ultimatums communicate to a PDA nervous system: you are required to perform in order to retain my relationship with you. The relationship is conditional. The conditions are demand-heavy. That communication is the opposite of what builds capacity. It is the opposite of everything this framework is designed to create.

"Is this PDA or are they manipulating me?"

Most parents are ashamed to ask this question. You are not alone in it.

PDA involves sophisticated avoidance strategies that can look, from the outside, exactly like manipulation. Elaborate excuses. Last-minute avoidance of things they agreed to. Apparent compliance followed by non-delivery. Using your care for them as a lever for getting out of demands. The behavior can appear calculated. The question of whether it is intentional is completely fair.

The distinction is the nervous system state driving it.

Manipulation, in the clinical sense, implies conscious, strategic exploitation of another person for personal benefit. The person evaluates the situation, identifies a vulnerability, and uses it deliberately to get what they want.

PDA avoidance is a threat response. An automatic, below-conscious-awareness mobilization of whatever tools are available to reduce the perceived threat. The strategies may be sophisticated. The person's nervous system has had years to develop them. Sophistication does not indicate deliberation. It indicates practice. A well-developed threat response is still a threat response, even when it looks strategic.

The practical difference: manipulation changes when consequences make it less effective. If a behavior is truly strategic and you attach a consequence that outweighs the benefit, the behavior changes. PDA avoidance does not change in response to consequences because it is not a cost-benefit calculation. It is a nervous system response. Consequences confirm the threat, produce more avoidance, and damage the relationship without changing the behavior.

If you have tried consequences repeatedly and the avoidance has not decreased (or has increased) that is your answer. You are not dealing with manipulation. You are dealing with a threat response that consequences cannot reach.

There is a third category worth naming. Some behaviors that look like PDA avoidance are driven by other things: depression (cannot get out of bed because the energy is not there, not because the demand is threatening), trauma responses (avoidance driven by trauma triggers rather than demand sensitivity), or oppositional patterns that formed over years of high-demand, high-conflict interaction and have taken on a life of their own. Clinical assessment by someone who actually understands PDA can help distinguish these. But the practical response to all of them is more similar than different: reduce the demand load, maintain connection, and create the conditions in which something different becomes possible.

"When do I stop?"

When do you stop accommodating? Stop adjusting? Stop being available at 2 AM? Stop carrying the weight of this?

The honest answer is: you do not stop. This is a neurological profile, not a phase. The demand sensitivity does not resolve. It can be managed, accommodated, understood, and worked with. The capacity can grow. The window can widen. The relationship can become the kind of relationship that supports a life worth living. But the underlying sensitivity does not go away.

What changes is what the work looks like. With a young child, the work is constant environmental management. With a teenager, the work shifts to presence, availability, and released control. With an adult child, the work shifts again to support without management, connection without agenda, and the gradual transfer of the framework from something you do for them to something they understand about themselves.

The work also changes as you change. As your own burnout is addressed. As your own patterns are recognized. As your nervous system becomes more stable and your capacity to sustain the approach increases. The framework does not get easier in the sense that the demands disappear. It gets easier in the sense that you get better at it. Your awareness sharpens. Your patterns quiet. Your repair comes faster. The lever steadies.

But you cannot sustain this from an empty system. So the real question is not "when do I stop" but "how do I sustain it." Chapter 13 (burnout) and Chapter 17 (your identity) address this directly and they apply at this stage with more urgency than at any other.

You need other people who understand. Not to fix it. To hold it alongside you. You need your own regulation practices, maintained even when time and energy are scarce. And you need permission to not be okay. To be struggling with this. To not have made your peace with it yet.

The work requires your presence. Not your performed resolution.

PART FIVE

Closing

You started this book probably exhausted. You are probably still exhausted.

But something may have shifted. Not a solution. Not a fix. Something quieter than that. A way of seeing what is happening in your child, in your home, in yourself, that makes it possible to respond differently. That shift is not small. It is the thing that changes everything else, slowly, over time.

You know what demand sensitivity is. You know the three mechanisms that drive your child's response. You know what it looks like, why nothing else has worked, and why you are not a bad parent for struggling with this.

You have a framework. Six pillars that target the nervous system, not the behavior. A crisis protocol for the moments when everything goes sideways. Eight scenarios that meet you in the situations you actually live with. A playbook you can flip to at 7:30 AM when you need words, not theory.

You have looked at yourself honestly. Your burnout. Your patterns. Your capacity for repair. Not because you are the problem, but because you are the lever, and a steady lever works better than a shaky one.

You have the long game. The team. The partner. The family. The teen years, if you are in them or heading toward them. The fears that keep you up at night, answered honestly rather than with reassurance that does not hold.

None of this will be perfect. You will fall into the compliance loop tomorrow morning. You will catch the empathy-demand sequence after the "but" has already landed. You will lose your temper and repair late and doubt whether any of this is working. That is the reality of this work. It is not linear. It is not clean. It does not look like progress most days.

But the nervous system is tracking. Yours and theirs. Every deposit. Every repair. Every moment you showed up without agenda. Every demand you dropped that did not need to be held. Every time you read the window and responded to what you saw instead of what you wanted. That evidence accumulates. It builds below the surface, in the nervous system's ledger, where the accounting is honest even when the day was not.

The morning that took three cycles and twenty-five minutes in month one takes one cycle and eight minutes in month four. Not because your child changed. Because the relational environment became demonstrably safe. That is the trajectory. Not perfection. Shift.

You are the lever. And you are still here.

Appendix: Reference, Tools, and Resources

Everything in this appendix is designed to be used, not just read. Print the quick reference cards and put them where you will see them during the hard moments. Complete the worksheets when your window is wide enough to hold them. Return to the word bank when you need language and your own words are not available.

The tools are numbered by the chapter they connect to. The text throughout the book points you here by name when a tool is relevant.

The Six Pillars at Home

RELATE

R — **Relationship**

Connect without agenda. Deposit before you withdraw. One intentional moment of low-demand connection per day.

E — **Empathy**

See the world through their nervous system. Perspective-taking that shifts your state. Empathy without "but."

L — **Lower Demands**

Reduce to what the system can handle today. Declarative language. "The toothbrush is on the counter."

A — **Adjust**

Personalize every strategy. Interest bridges, not bribes. What works Tuesday may not work Wednesday.

T — **Time**

More time than seems reasonable. Then add more. No clock references. Recovery is non-negotiable.

E — **Environment**

Physical, sensory, and social conditions that support nervous system safety. You are the most important variable.

Start with two: Relationship and Lower Demands.

The ADAPT Protocol

IN-THE-MOMENT CRISIS RESPONSE

A

Assess

Read their body first: escalating or shutting down? Then read yours. Jaw tight? Heart racing? Breathe first. Sit down.

D

Decrease

Stop talking. Step back. Sit down. Drop the demand. Drop all demands. Remove time pressure. Less is more. Nothing is often best.

A

Align

Return their sense of control. Genuine choices only. "You're in charge of what happens next." Only say it if it is true.

P

Pace

Wait. Be present and quiet. Do not fill the silence. Do not ask "are you okay?" The silence is the intervention.

T

Test

Smallest possible next thing. "I'm making toast, want some?" If the answer is no: wait more. "Not yet" is useful data.

ADAPT is cyclical. You will cycle through the steps multiple times. That is accurate responsiveness, not failure.

Is the Window Open or Closed?

A 10-SECOND READ BEFORE ANY INTERACTION

OPEN

They can think flexibly. They can tolerate some discomfort. They can engage with you even if they do not want to.

Parent. Hold the expectation warmly.

NARROWING

Shorter responses. Tension building. Increased rigidity. Still partly accessible but losing flexibility.

Reduce. Drop non-essentials. Slow down.

CLOSED

Thinking brain offline. Capacity genuinely unavailable. Meltdown or shutdown territory.

Stop demands entirely. ADAPT protocol.

Not sure? Try the smallest version. Their response tells you where they are.

The (Re)Pair Spectrum

MATCH THE REPAIR TO THE WINDOW

Ambient *Window closed*	No words. Food placed nearby. Sit in the room. Exist without requiring anything. Your presence, without agenda, is the repair.
Physical *Window opening*	Proximity and warmth. No language about the rupture. A hand on their shoulder if tolerated. Sit near. Receive their lean without escalating.
Named *Window partially open*	One sentence. "I came in too hard this morning." Then silence. No follow-up. No "are we okay?" The sentence is the repair.
Conversational *Window wide open*	Brief exchange. "Can I ask what that felt like from where you were?" Then actually listen. Not to defend. To understand.

The right repair is the one their window can hold right now.

Playbook Key Phrases

WHAT TO SAY WHEN YOU NEED IT MOST

DURING A MELTDOWN

"I'm here." • "There's no rush." • "You don't have to talk."

"We don't need to figure this out right now."

"Nothing needs to happen right now."

DURING SHUTDOWN

"I'm in the next room if you need me."

"There's food on the counter." • "No rush."

Or say nothing at all. Place water within reach.

WHEN THEY REFUSE

"The toothbrush is on the counter." • "Your shoes are by the door."

"Is there a version of this that would work?"

"This needs to happen today. You get to decide when and how."

AFTER YOU LOSE YOUR TEMPER

"I pushed too hard earlier. I'm sorry. You don't need to say anything."

"That wasn't okay. I was frustrated and I put that on you."

FOR YOURSELF

"Connection, not compliance." • "I am the lever, not the problem."

"Regulate first. Everything else comes after."

"They are not giving me a hard time. They are having a hard time."

During a Meltdown

THE CRISIS — ADAPT TRIAGE

CHECK YOURSELF FIRST

Before you do anything else. Jaw tight? Heart pounding? Urgency in your chest? You are activated. Three seconds. Unclench your jaw. Drop your shoulders. Sit down. You go first.

ADAPT FOR THIS MOMENT

A **Assess**
Read their body. Escalating (tense, loud, moving) or at peak (rigid, screaming, unreachable)? You do not intervene at peak. You hold steady and wait for the shift.

D **Decrease**
Stop talking. Step back. Get lower than them. Drop the demand that triggered this. Drop every other demand. Remove the audience. Remove time pressure.

A **Align**
Not yet. During active meltdown, do not offer choices. The system cannot process options at peak. Align comes after the shift.

P **Pace**
This is where you spend most of a meltdown. Present. Quiet. Not filling the silence. The stress hormones need time to clear. You cannot speed that process.

T **Test**
When you see the shift (posture softening, breathing deepening): try the smallest possible next thing. Not the original demand. If silence, wait more.

DURING THE CRISIS: TRY TO AVOID

"Calm down."
A demand to regulate a system that cannot regulate on command.

"Use your words."
Language production is offline.

"You're okay."
Invalidation. Their system is telling them they are not.

"What happened?"
Demands retrieval and narration from a brain in survival mode.

"If you don't stop..."
A threat layered on top of a threat.

"We talked about this."
Requires memory retrieval. Carries implicit shame.

The meltdown has a physiological arc. Waiting is the intervention.

During a Meltdown

THE RETURN — WHEN THE WINDOW REOPENS

SIGNS THE WINDOW IS REOPENING

- Posture shifts from rigid to softened or curled
- Breathing deepens and slows
- Screaming transitions to crying, then to quiet
- They make eye contact or look toward you
- A word or two appears, even just a sound
- They physically move closer or reach for you

NOW: WHAT TO SAY

One phrase, said once, quietly. Then wait. You are offering a single signal of safety.

"I'm here."	*Presence without demand.*
"There's no rush."	*Removes time pressure.*
"We don't need to figure this out right now."	*Removes the expectation of resolution.*
"I'm not going anywhere."	*Commitment without agenda.*

WHAT TO DO NOW	WHAT NOT TO DO

Test with something tiny: toast, water, a blanket.	Immediately revisit the triggering demand.
Stay physically available without pursuing.	Process: "What happened?" "Why?"
Match the energy of any bid they make.	Lecture or reference it as a teaching moment.
Let them set the pace for returning.	Require an apology or acknowledgment.
File what worked. Use it next time.	Pretend nothing happened if they want to talk.

RELATE PILLARS GOING FORWARD

R The next hour is a deposit opportunity. Be near without agenda.

E Later, if the window is wide: "That looked really hard." No "but."

L Keep the rest of the day low-demand. The budget is spent.

T Recovery takes longer than you think. Do not rush the return.

E Lower sensory input for the next few hours. Quiet space. Fewer people.

During Shutdown

THE CRISIS — ADAPT TRIAGE

WHAT'S HAPPENING

Shutdown is different from meltdown. The energy is down, not up. The nervous system has decided that fighting and fleeing are not available and has collapsed into conservation mode. Flat affect. Silence. Stillness. Glazed eyes. Withdrawal. They may appear calm from the outside. They are not calm. They are in freeze.

CHECK YOURSELF FIRST

Shutdown can trigger your anxiety because nothing visible is happening. The urge to fix, to engage, to pull them out of it is strong. That urge is a demand. Check your state. Breathe. Your job is to reduce input, not increase it.

ADAPT FOR THIS MOMENT

A **Assess**
Read the freeze. Flat affect, silence, stillness, glazed eyes, absent responses. This is conservation mode. The system is overwhelmed and has gone offline. Do not try to bring them back.

D **Decrease**
Reduce sensory input. Lower the lights. Turn off noise. Reduce the number of people in the space. Every sensory input is load on a system that is already past capacity.

A **Align**
Their body is telling you what they need: less. Align by reducing your presence if it is adding to the load. Some children need a person nearby. Some need to be alone. Read which one yours needs right now.

P **Pace**
Shutdown can last minutes or hours. The timeline is not yours to set. Do not check in every ten minutes. Each check-in is a demand. Let the recovery happen at the pace the nervous system requires.

T **Test**

Place food or water within reach without comment. Do not bring it with eye contact and a "here you go." Set it down. Walk away. If they engage with it, the window is beginning to open.

DURING THE CRISIS: TRY TO AVOID

"What's wrong?"

A demand to identify, articulate, and share their internal state.

"Talk to me."

A direct demand for verbal production from a system that has taken it offline.

"You can't just sit there."

A demand to produce visible activity. Freeze is a nervous system state, not a choice.

"We need to deal with this."

A demand to engage while in conservation mode.

"How can I help?"

Sounds compassionate. Requires them to assess needs, identify solutions, formulate a response.

Shutdown is not a strategy. It is a nervous system state. They will come back when the system allows it.

During Shutdown

THE RETURN — WHEN THE WINDOW REOPENS

SIGNS THE WINDOW IS REOPENING

- Shoulders drop, jaw relaxes, hands unclench
- Breathing deepens visibly
- They shift position or move after being still
- They engage with food or water you placed nearby
- A word or sound, even a sigh
- They look at you or toward a shared space

NOW: WHAT TO SAY

Almost nothing. The system is recovering. One short phrase or none at all. Quiet presence may be all that is needed.

"I'm in the next room if you need me."	*Available without hovering.*
"There's food on the counter."	*Meets a need without requiring them to come to you.*
"No rush."	*Two words. Removes time pressure.*
Say nothing at all.	*Leave water within reach. Leave the room if your presence adds load.*

WHAT TO DO NOW	WHAT NOT TO DO

Place food and water within reach without comment.

Be nearby but not in the room if proximity adds demand.

Lower lights, reduce noise, minimize sensory input.

Let them re-engage on their own terms and timeline.

Receive any bid (a word, a look, moving closer) without intensity.

Pursue them. Knock repeatedly. Open their door.

Set a timer on recovery. "Fifteen minutes and then..."

Require them to come out for meals.

Interpret shutdown as manipulation or avoidance.

Flood them with relief when they re-emerge.

RELATE PILLARS GOING FORWARD

R When they re-emerge, match their energy. Low-key. No big reaction.

E Do not process. If the window opens wide later: "That looked heavy."

L The rest of the day is recovery. Drop everything non-essential.

T Shutdown recovery takes longer than meltdown recovery. Plan for hours, not minutes.

E Keep the environment quiet. The nervous system is rebuilding capacity from zero.

When They Refuse

THE APPROACH — READING THE WINDOW

WHAT'S HAPPENING

They are not choosing to defy you. Their nervous system has encountered a demand that exceeds the current window. The threat-detection system has activated. What you see as refusal is the system protecting itself from overload. The demand may be objectively small. The capacity available right now may also be small.

CHECK YOURSELF FIRST

Ask the key question: what would actually happen if this did not happen right now? If the answer is nothing dangerous, you have room. If it is non-negotiable (safety, medication), clear the deck around it. Either way, check your urgency. Is it real or habitual?

ADAPT FOR THIS MOMENT

A **Assess**

Read the window. Narrowing or closed? If narrowing, you have room to try a different approach. If closed, the demand is not happening right now. That is data, not failure.

D **Decrease**

Switch from direct commands to declarative language. "The toothbrush is on the counter" instead of "go brush your teeth." Reduce the demand to its smallest possible version. Half the task. A different method. A different time.

A **Align**

Give genuine choices. "Is there a version of this that would work?" "What would make this easier?" Only if the answers are genuinely available. If only yes is acceptable, do not ask.

P **Pace**
Give it time. Walk away. Come back later. The demand did not disappear. It moved to a wider window. Ten minutes of waiting costs less than ten minutes of escalation.

T **Test**
Try an interest bridge. Embed the demand inside something familiar. Modify the method. If nothing moves, release it. Try again tomorrow.

DURING THE REFUSAL: TRY TO AVOID

"Just do it and it'll be over."
Minimizes the difficulty. Communicates you do not understand why this is hard.

"But you did it yesterday."
The capacity assumption. Yesterday's nervous system is not today's.

"I'm not asking much."
You are not the judge. Their nervous system is.

"You need to do this."
The word "need" is a red flag for a demand sensitive system.

Repeating the demand.
Each repetition doubles the load. One ask, then wait.

Adding consequences.
Now they are managing the demand plus the threat of loss. Two demands, neither met.

The question is not "how do I make them do it?" It is "what does the window need to hold this?"

When They Refuse

THE FRAMEWORK — RELATE IN ACTION

DECLARATIVE LANGUAGE BANK

Same information, radically different demand load. Place information in the environment and let their system decide.

INSTEAD OF THIS	TRY THIS
"Go brush your teeth."	"The toothbrush is on the counter."
"Come eat."	"Breakfast is on the table."
"Get ready to go."	"The car is ready when you are."
"Put your jacket on."	"Your jacket is on the hook."
"Do your homework."	"The homework folder is on the table."
"Go to bed."	"Your room is ready when you are."

IF THE DEMAND IS NON-NEGOTIABLE

Some demands cannot be dropped. Safety. Essential medication. Medical procedures. When the demand is truly non-negotiable, everything else around it becomes the intervention.

"This needs to happen today. You get to decide when and how."	*Honest about the requirement. Autonomy over process.*
"What would make this easier?"	*Genuine question. Accept "nothing" as data.*
"Would it help if I did part of it?"	*Offer to share the load.*
"Is there a version of this that would work?"	*Opens negotiation on terms.*

RELATE PILLARS IN PLAY

- **R** Protect the relationship over the task. The task will come back. Trust compounds.
- **E** "Something about this is really overwhelming right now." No "but."
- **L** Can you do half? A different method? A different time? Reduce to the essential.
- **A** Use an interest bridge. Adjust the communication channel. Text, note, indirect language.
- **T** Give it time. Walk away. Come back in ten minutes. The demand moved, it did not disappear.
- **E** Is the environment adding load? Noise, lights, audience, the room itself?

After You Lose Your Temper

YOUR CRISIS — REGULATE FIRST

WHAT'S HAPPENING

You yelled. You said something you did not mean. You escalated when you knew you should not have. It happened. You cannot undo it. Your nervous system was outside its window and your patterns fired before your awareness caught up. That is not a character judgment. It is a nervous system event. What you do next matters more than what you just did.

REGULATE YOURSELF FIRST

You cannot repair from activation. If your system is still hot, the repair will carry the residue of the rupture. Leave the room if you can. Breathe. Give yourself the same grace you are learning to give your child. You are a person with a nervous system that has a budget. Yours was depleted. That is real.

DO NOT REPAIR YET

The urge to repair immediately is about your discomfort, not their readiness. If your child is still activated or shut down, the repair is another demand. It requires them to receive your words, process the apology, and generate a response. Wait. The timing belongs to their nervous system, not your guilt.

WHILE YOU WAIT: SELF-TALK

"I am human. My patterns fired. That is not the end of the story."

"What I do next matters more than what I just did."

"I cannot repair from this state. Regulate first."

"They do not need me to be perfect. They need me to come back."

"The relationship is not ruined. Ruptures happen. Repair builds."

"I can try again. That option is always available to me."

THE (RE)PAIR SPECTRUM: MATCH THE REPAIR TO THE WINDOW

Ambient *Window closed*	No words. Be in the house. Place food nearby. Exist without requiring anything.
Physical *Window opening*	Proximity and warmth. No language about the rupture. Sit near. Receive their lean.
Named *Window partially open*	One sentence. "I came in too hard. I'm sorry." Then silence. No follow-up.
Conversational *Window wide open*	"Can I ask what that felt like?" Then actually listen. Not to defend. To understand.

After You Lose Your Temper

THE REPAIR — WHAT TO SAY AND WHAT NOT TO SAY

WHEN THE WINDOW OPENS: REPAIR LANGUAGE

Specific. Owned. No justification. No expectation of response. The repair is something you offer, not a transaction.

"I pushed too hard earlier. I'm sorry. You don't need to say anything."	*Names it. Owns it. Removes the demand to respond.*
"That wasn't okay. I was frustrated and I put that on you."	*No "but." No shared blame.*
"I can see that what I did made things harder."	*Validates their experience of the rupture.*
"I got caught up in the schedule and forgot you needed more time."	*Specific. Shows you know what happened.*
"I think I made that feel like you had no choice. I'm working on that."	*Commitment to change, not just apology.*

TRY TO AVOID THESE

"I'm sorry, but you weren't listening."
The "but" redirects blame. Cancels the apology.

"I said I'm sorry, can we move on?"
A demand for closure. Your need, not theirs.

"Are we okay?"
A demand for reassurance that the relationship survived.

"I'm sorry you felt that way."
Not an apology. Does not own anything.

"I already apologized."
Weaponized repair. Communicates their response is unreasonable.

WHAT TO DO	WHAT NOT TO DO
Wait for their timeline, not your guilt.	Require them to apologize back.
Repair without requiring their participation.	Process it as a couple in front of them.
Change the behavior over time. Words are the beginning. Behavior is the proof.	Use the repair as a teaching moment.
Accept their repair in whatever form it comes: a look, sitting closer, humor.	Withdraw into guilt and become emotionally unavailable.

Verbal repair followed by behavioral repetition is not repair. Changed behavior over time is the proof.

For Yourself

YOUR NERVOUS SYSTEM — THE LEVER

WHAT'S HAPPENING

You are the most powerful variable in your child's environment. Not because you caused their demand sensitivity. Because of all the variables in the equation, you are the one most responsive to change. Your state is what their nervous system encounters first. A steady lever works better than a shaky one. This page is about steadying the lever.

THE 30-SECOND CHECK

Before any interaction. Before the morning routine. Before addressing the homework. Before responding to the meltdown. Ask: will this go better if I take 30 seconds first? If your jaw is tight, your heart is racing, or urgency is running: the answer is yes. Breathe. Unclench. Slow down. Then go.

WHERE ARE YOU RIGHT NOW?

ACTIVATED

Tense. Irritable. Racing thoughts. Urgency. Jaw clenched. Short fuse. Startling easily.

You need to regulate before engaging. Three seconds minimum. More if available.

IN YOUR WINDOW

Thinking clearly. Present. Flexible. Able to feel something other than anxiety or exhaustion.

Go. You have capacity. Protect this.

SHUTDOWN

Numb. Flat. Going through the motions. Checked out. Unable to access joy.

You need rest, support, or relief before you can be the lever. This is not weakness. This is depletion.

SELF-TALK FOR THE HARD MOMENTS

Pick three. Say them out loud ten times. They will be available to you under stress if you have practiced them when you did not need them.

"This is a hard moment, not a crisis."

"Connection, not compliance."

"I am the lever, not the problem."

"Their behavior is a signal, not an attack."

"Regulate first. Everything else comes after."

"I don't have to fix this. I have to survive it without making it worse."

"They are not giving me a hard time. They are having a hard time."

For Yourself

SUSTAINING — PLAYS FOR THE LONG GAME

WHAT YOU ACTUALLY NEED

Not baths and candles. These.

Another regulated adult who gets it

Someone who knows what PDA is. Someone whose nervous system does not add to your load. Someone you do not have to translate for before you can exhale.

Genuine respite

Not respite where you are on call by text. Respite where you are unreachable. Where you can set your nervous system down for a few hours. Extraordinarily hard to arrange. Non-negotiable for sustainability.

Permission to grieve

The grief does not resolve. It comes back. You need a space where it is allowed to come back without being redirected toward gratitude or silver linings.

Professional support for you

Not to learn more strategies. To have a space where someone is tracking your nervous system state with the same care you give your child's.

YOUR DEMAND AUDIT

For each demand on your life, ask:

Did I choose this, or did it just accumulate?

What would actually happen if I lowered or released it?

Is it serving my family right now, or a version of my life that no longer exists?

ONE THING THIS WEEK

You do not need to overhaul your life. Pick one demand you can release this week. Not forever. For now. See what the room feels like. That room is the space in which the lever works.

You are not the problem. You are the most powerful lever available. A problem is something to be fixed. A lever is something to be used.

Worksheets

PRINTABLE TOOLS FOR DAILY USE

Tool 1: My Nervous System Right Now

Chapter 12

○ **ACTIVATED**	Tense. Irritable. Racing thoughts. Urgency. Jaw clenched. Short fuse.
○ **IN MY WINDOW**	Thinking clearly. Present. Flexible. Able to feel.
○ **SHUTDOWN**	Numb. Flat. Going through the motions. Checked out.

What shifted me here:

What I need right now:

The 30-second question: will the next ten minutes go better if I take thirty seconds first?

Tool 2: Personal Demand Audit

Chapter 13

List the demands your life is placing on you outside of parenting:

1.

2.

3. ______________________________

4. ______________________________

5. ______________________________

6. ______________________________

7. ______________________________

8. ______________________________

For each one, ask:

Did I choose this, or did it just accumulate?

What would actually happen if I lowered or released it?

Is it serving my family now, or a version of my life that no longer exists?

One demand I can release this week:

____

____

Tool 3: 24-Hour Demand Snapshot

Chapter 8

Track every demand your child encounters across a full day. Include explicit (things you say), implicit (things you expect), and invisible (body language, sensory environment, social expectations).

Morning routine

Meals

Transitions

School-related

Hygiene

Social expectations

Bedtime

Other

Total demands in 24 hours:

Genuinely non-negotiable:

Could be modified:

Could be released:

What surprised you most?

Tool 4: My Child's PDA Profile

Chapter 3

Child's name:

Date:

Hardest demands for my child:

Window widest at:

Window narrowest at:

Current intense interests:

Sensory inputs that help regulate:

Sensory inputs that make things worse:

____

____

What shutdown looks like for my child:

____

____

What escalation looks like:

____

____

Communication that works best right now:

____

____

Tool 5: One-Page Summary for Your Child's Team

Chapter 16

Print this and bring it to every meeting about your child.

Child's name:

Age:

What helps my child feel safe:

What makes things harder:

Current intense interests (regulation tools, not rewards):

Biggest demand triggers:

When escalating, my child looks like:

When shutting down, my child looks like:

What to do when this happens:

What NOT to do:

Best way to communicate with my child:

Parent/caregiver contact:

Glossary of Key Terms

ADAPT. The five-step crisis protocol for in-the-moment response: Assess, Decrease, Align, Pace, Test. Designed to help the nervous system return to the window of tolerance without adding threat.

Autonomy threat. The nervous system's response to perceived loss of control. One of the three mechanisms driving the demand-threat response in PDA. Demands constrain choice. Constrained choice is experienced as a survival-level threat.

Capacity assumption. The pattern of expecting today's capacity to match yesterday's. "But they did it yesterday." A common demand-placing pattern that adds relational threat on top of the demand itself.

Co-regulation. The biological process by which one nervous system influences another. Operates constantly through channels faster than language: facial expression, muscle tension, vocal pitch, breathing rate, posture. Your state affects their state. Not a technique. Physics.

Compliance loop. The pattern of repeating a demand with increasing pressure. Each repetition doubles the demand load. Breaking the loop: one ask, then wait.

Declarative language. Placing information in the environment without requiring compliance. "The toothbrush is on the counter" instead of "go brush your teeth." Same information, radically different demand load.

Demand audit. The process of identifying and counting all demands (explicit, implicit, and invisible) in a given period. Makes the invisible visible. Most parents are stunned by the total.

Demand budget. The finite amount of demand a nervous system can hold before it depletes. Every demand is a withdrawal. Sleep, safety, autonomy, and regulation are deposits. When the budget is empty, even small demands produce large responses.

Demand sensitivity. A nervous system that is more reactive to demands as a stimulus. The operational term for the PDA profile. Parallels sensory sensitivity. Names the mechanism rather than the behavior.

Empathy-demand sequence. The pattern of following empathy with a demand. "I know this is hard, but we still need to get dressed." The "but" cancels the empathy. Over time, teaches the child that empathy predicts pressure.

Explicit demands. Demands you can hear yourself saying. "Put your shoes on." "Do your homework." The visible layer.

Implicit demands. Unstated but expected. The assumption that they will sit at the table. The unspoken rule about screen time. The child's nervous system tracks these.

Interest bridge. Using a child's current interest to make a demand more tolerable. The interest is present alongside the demand, not offered as a reward after compliance. Different from a bribe.

Interest colonization. When a special interest becomes associated with demands through overuse as a bridge, causing the child to begin avoiding the interest itself.

Intolerance of Uncertainty (IU). Elevated sensitivity to uncertainty. Every demand carries unknowns. For someone with high IU, each unknown is amplified into threat. A stronger predictor of PDA traits than anxiety alone.

Invisible demands. Demands you have not consciously identified as demands. Your body language communicating urgency. The ambient pressure of a tidy house. The emotional expectation that they be in a better mood.

Masking. Suppressing demand avoidance in environments where the person does not feel safe enough to show it. The cost is paid later, usually at home. "School says fine. Home says otherwise."

PDA (Pathological Demand Avoidance). The clinical term for a profile in which the nervous system responds to everyday demands with extreme avoidance driven by anxiety. Most commonly seen within the autism spectrum. Also known as Persistent Demand Avoidance or Pervasive Drive for Autonomy.

(Re)Pair. Repair through presence rather than words. Reconnecting the relationship after a rupture by being available, without demanding engagement. The Bluetooth metaphor: bring the devices into range, make sure both are discoverable, and let the connection re-establish on its own.

RELATE. The six-pillar clinical intervention framework for PDA: Relationship, Empathy, Lower Demands, Adjust, Time, Environment. Developed by Rachelle Manco, LCSW, and Justin Manco, CMHC.

Subcortical threat detection. The brain's threat-detection system, centered in the amygdala, that processes demands as threats before conscious awareness. The nervous system has already responded before the person knows they are responding.

Window of tolerance. The zone of nervous system arousal within which flexible thinking, connection, and responsive action are possible. Outside this window, these capacities are genuinely inaccessible. For demand sensitive individuals, the window is often narrow and easily destabilized by demands.

Resources

These resources are provided for reference. Inclusion does not constitute endorsement by BSPUTAH, LLC.

From the RELATE Framework

RELATE Foundational Training Manual. The complete clinical intervention framework this book is built on. Written for professionals who work with PDA individuals. relatepda.com/manual

Live Team Training. Training for schools, treatment centers, and clinical teams. Customized to your setting and population. relatepda.com/training

Clinical Consultation. Individual sessions for families and professionals. relatepda.com

PDA Organizations

PDA Society (UK). The leading international resource for PDA information, research updates, and community. pdasociety.org.uk

PDA North America. U.S.-based PDA advocacy, education, and parent community. pdanorthamerica.org

Crisis Resources

988 Suicide and Crisis Lifeline. Call or text 988. Available 24/7.

Crisis Text Line. Text HOME to 741741.

Emergency Services. Call 911 or go to your nearest emergency room.

About the Authors

Rachelle Manco, LCSW and **Justin Manco, CMHC** are licensed clinicians specializing in autism and co-occurring conditions, including PDA, anxiety, OCD, sensory processing differences, and trauma. They work in residential treatment and intensive outpatient settings with complex neurodivergent populations: the individuals whose presentations are the most misunderstood and the most poorly served by standard approaches.

The RELATE framework was developed from direct clinical work with PDA individuals and the families, educators, and teams who support them. It exists because nothing else did. No structured intervention framework. No clinical training manual. No implementation protocol for PDA existed anywhere in the field. RELATE is the first.

Rachelle and Justin operate under BSPUTAH, LLC. Their work, including the clinical manual, this book, live training, and clinical consultation, is available at relatepda.com.

Notes

Notes

Notes

Notes

Notes

www.ingramcontent.com/pod-product-compliance
Lightning Source LLC
LaVergne TN
LVHW010646110826
845149LV00014B/2974

* 9 7 9 8 9 9 5 2 8 8 1 4 5 *